Race in American Musical Theater

Forthcoming in the series:

Hip-Hop in Musical Theater by Nicole Hodges Persley
Queer Approaches in Musical Theatre by Ryan Donovan

Race in American Musical Theater

Josephine Lee

methuen | drama

LONDON • NEW YORK • OXFORD • NEW DELHI • SYDNEY

METHUEN DRAMA
Bloomsbury Publishing Plc
50 Bedford Square, London, WC1B 3DP, UK
1385 Broadway, New York, NY 10018, USA
29 Earlsfort Terrace, Dublin 2, Ireland

First published in Great Britain 2023

Series design by Rebecca Heselton

A catalog record for this book is available from the British Library.

Library of Congress Cataloging-in-Publication Data

Names: Lee, Josephine, 1960- author.
Title: Race in American musical theatre / Josephine Lee.
Description: London ; New York : Methuen Drama, 2023. | Series: Topics in
musical theatre | Includes bibliographical references and index. |
Identifiers: LCCN 2022053023 | ISBN 9781350248212 (paperback) |
ISBN 9781350248236 (epub) | ISBN 9781350248229 (pdf)
Subjects: LCSH: Musicals–United States–History and criticism. |
Music and race–United States.
Classification: LCC ML2054 .L43 2023 | DDC 782.1/40973–dc23/eng/20221213
LC record available at https://lccn.loc.gov/2022053023

ISBN: PB: 978-1-3502-4821-2
ePDF: 978-1-3502-4822-9
eBook: 978-1-3502-4823-6

Series: Topics in Musical Theatre

Typeset by Deanta Global Publishing Services, Chennai, India
Printed and bound in Great Britain

To find out more about our authors and books visit www.bloomsbury.com and sign
up for our newsletters.

Contents

Introduction
American Musical Theater and Its Discontents

Whether performed on Broadway, in a community theater, or a high school, musicals are a well-established tradition in the United States. Too often dismissed as light entertainment that offers little food for thought, musical theater arouses strong emotions and can convey powerful ideas. This book serves as an introduction to how race matters in American musical theater. A complex creative form involving narrative, song, dance, and design, musical theater blends the more *representational* aspects of theater—its ability to reflect the world offstage—with *presentational* elements such as spectacle, music, and dance. Race becomes significant both in how musicals represent characters and stories and also in how they present what is unique to the stage.

Sociologists Michael Omi and Howard Winant have offered important ways of understanding race as foundational to American politics and culture. Social hierarchies based on race change through time, yet what they call "racial formation" remains consistent in how people view themselves and interact with one another. Based on physical attributes, racial identities are "made up" forms of difference, social constructions used as a "way to navigate in the social world—to situate ourselves and others in the context of social hierarchies, to discern friend from foe, and to provide a guide to social action with other individuals and groups." But although race is socially constructed, it is far from purely imaginary. "Made up" categories of race affect how our bodies "are visually read, understood and narrated by means of symbolic meanings and association."[1] In the United States, how much freedom, wealth, or power someone has always depended on race. Racial distinctions undergirded laws that determined whether someone counted as citizen, slave, or alien. Race affected where people lived and traveled, who could own land and property, whom one could marry, who had access to education, and who could testify in court. Similarly, race has always been a determining factor in who performs in or attends American musical theater and what is laughed at, reveled in, and applauded on the stage. Musicals provide glimpses of the ideologies of colonization, slavery, segregation, exclusion, and xenophobia. Sadly, even beloved works were created and produced in highly segregated spaces and sometimes perpetuate racist perspectives.

Like other forms of theater, musical theater relies on repetition—the imitation of characters, stories, and devices from other works, the training and rehearsal of performers, nightly performances, and revivals of earlier productions. The repetition of a racial stereotype or cross-racial casting can become especially problematic. One example appears in *Avenue Q* (2003), a show featuring a mix of humans and puppets satirizing American urban life and sexuality that includes the character Christmas Eve, a Japanese immigrant speaking heavily accented English. Stephen Quigley has described his response to a 2014 Greenville, South Carolina production: "The sight was redolent of Mickey Rooney playing the character Mr. Yunioshi in *Breakfast at Tiffany's*, but in this case the [white] actress, in pajamas, heavy eye makeup, and with hair sticks spiking out of her hair bun talked and sang with a high choppy tonal dialect short on prepositions."[2] Quigley notes the song "Everyone's a Little Bit Racist," which makes the case that because people themselves harbor a degree of racism, they should not be so sensitive around racist remarks:

> Everyone's a little bit racist
> It's true.
> But everyone is just about
> As racist as you!
> If we all could just admit
> That we are racist a little bit,
> And everyone stopped being
> So PC
> Maybe we could live in—
> Harmony!

Quigley's attention is caught by "the one woman of Asian descent in the audience," who is "about the same age as Christmas Eve," and how she responds to Christmas Eve and the song's assumption that "everyone" has experienced racism equally.

> Instead of watching Christmas Eve sing-song her parts on the stage, I found myself watching this audience member

and how she reacted to "Eveyone's a rittre bit lacist!" and "I know you are no intending to be, but carring me 'Olientarr' . . . offensive to me!" Yes, this audience member did smile and nod at some of the jokes, but there was also a great discomfort about her as well, and at times she looked away or failed to laugh—perhaps a realization that she was the Other in the room. The joke was on her.

Theater scholar Donatella Galella has described similar feelings of discomfort during the 2013 New York City Center Encores! production of *It's a Bird . . . It's a Plane . . . It's Superman*, a revival of the 1966 musical. The production featured clichéd "pentatonic music and anti-Asian jokes as the white Man of Steel battered the Chinese characters to save Metropolis," and presented yellowface versions of "the Flying Lings, Red Chinese acrobats" pitted against a white all-American hero.[3] For Galella, the production fostered "stereotypical Asianness through racialized makeup, hair, costume, accent, diction, gesture, movement, and music," an experience made even worse by the implicit expectation that audience members should respond to these stereotypes only as harmless fun. Galella, who identifies as Asian American, felt "indignant anger, profound sadness, and racial alienation" in stark contrast to the enjoyment of white audience members around her.

American musicals have not just elicited discontent about racist content. They have also been used to advocate for racial equality. From the nineteenth century on, theatrical productions and arts activists have openly challenged typecasting and showcased the talents of African American,

Native American, Latinx, and Asian American theater artists. In June 2020, Black, Indigenous, and People of Color theater makers signed the online letter, "We See You, White American Theater." Their protest of the white perspectives dominating American theater quickly added tens of thousands of signatures.[4] "We See You, White American Theater" asked for significant changes to programming, casting, training, and management, and cited reports that in 2017–18 only about 20 percent of shows on Off Broadway and Broadway stages were created by people of color, nearly two-thirds of roles were cast with white actors, and about 94 percent of directors were white.[5] The letter was an important reminder that the issues of race in American musical theater involve not only what is on stage but also who creates, watches, and profits from these representations.

Each of the following chapters covers a different aspect of race in American musical theater, but all have common aims. One is to provide historical background on musical theater and racial formation in order to contextualize how certain theatrical practices came into being. Another is to offer a multiracial and comparative approach that acknowledges the participation of African Americans, Asian Americans, Latinx, and other people of color in musical theater. The third is to examine particular examples that show how musicals, despite their reputation as light entertainment, serve as complicated and powerful forms of social conditioning.

The topic of race arouses anxiety and even resentment, especially when such discussions involve favorite musicals. More so than other theatergoers, musical theater audiences are regarded as nostalgia-loving and wary of change.

Sometimes a degree of familiarity, whether produced by habit, convenience, or pragmatism, drives decisions for what to produce or attend, and words of caution or criticism are feared as spoilers. David Savran once wrote of musical theater that "No theater form is as single-mindedly devoted to producing pleasure, inspiring spectators to tap their feet, sing along, or otherwise be carried away. This utopian—and mimetic—dimension of the musical (linked to its relentless reflexivity) makes it into a kind of hothouse for the manufacture of theatrical seduction and the ideological positions to which mass audiences can be seduced."[6] Suggesting that a musical can perpetuate racist attitudes or produce racial harm throws a brick through the glass of this hothouse. However, with a nod to Bertolt Brecht, we can look at the American musical not just as pleasure but as instruction.

Previews

Chapter 1 reflects upon the history of racial stereotypes in musical theater. How and why did different racial types, such as the comic Jim Crow, the savage "Injun," or the exotic "oriental," become so familiar onstage? What implicit messages do racial types carry about servitude, colonial conquest, and power? Racial stereotypes reduced people to objects of curiosity, derision, and desire in roles that were revived again and again. Chapter 1 includes now-forgotten eighteenth-century works such as Anne Julia Hatton's *Tammany; or, The Indian Chief* (1794) in addition to regularly revived favorites such as *Annie Get Your Gun* (1946), *Anything Goes* (1934), or *Oklahoma!* (1943).

Stereotypes go along with practices of cross-racial performance that give white actors the privilege of playing racial Others and deny performers of color the ability to represent themselves. White privilege restricted who was able to make, attend, or profit from much of the commercial enterprise of American musical theater. However, American musical theater has never been an all-white enterprise. Chapter 2 surveys the history of Black musicals, beginning in the late nineteenth century with *Peculiar Sam* (1879). Works such as *A Trip to Coontown* (1898) or *Shuffle Along* (1921) provided important alternatives to the white-dominated commercial theaters of Broadway fame. These musicals not only fostered separate spaces for Black theater artists and audiences but also commented meaningfully on Black agency, artistry, and community, issues examined again in later Broadway productions such as *Dreamgirls* (1981), *Jelly's Last Jam* (1992), and *Bring in 'da Noise, Bring in 'da Funk* (1995).

Of course, white theater artists have also focused on the problems of race. Chapter 3 looks closely at *Show Boat* (1927), *South Pacific* (1949), and *The King and I* (1951), musicals that highlight problems of bigotry and racial intolerance. Despite their liberal stance, however, these musicals relegated most Black and Asian characters to secondary roles, and their original Broadway productions continued practices of blackface and yellowface casting. This chapter ends with a closer look at *Flower Drum Song* as a notable contrast. Based on the best-selling novel by Chinese American writer C. Y. Lee, the 1958 production of *Flower Drum Song* had a mainly Asian American cast, a first on Broadway. It was also the only one of these musicals to have its libretto completely reworked for a Broadway revival in 2002. As rewritten by David Henry Hwang, the new *Flower Drum Song* offers a case study of how certain musicals might be revived not just as classics to be preserved, but as creatively reimagined theatrical experiences.

The first three chapters address how race influences the characterization and narratives in musicals. Chapter 4 makes clear that race helped shape another distinctive musical theater feature: the female chorus line. From the nineteenth century on, lavish displays associating white femininity with "good breeding" were regular aspects of musicals such as Ziegfeld's *Follies*. White ensembles also presented blackface and harem numbers, cross-racial acts providing sexual titillation and a touch of the exotic. However, white chorines were not the only ones drawing applause on the American musical stage. Black chorus lines in musicals such as *The Creole Show* (1890) used light-skinned African American women to play a variety of racial types, and the superlative skills of Black dancers in musicals such as *Shuffle Along* set a new standard for choreography. Chapter 4 concludes by discussing how race was addressed in the 1975 Broadway hit *A Chorus Line*. Inspired by personal interviews with Broadway dancers, *A Chorus Line* foregrounded racial identity as integral to the experience of performing in musical theater as well as to offstage life. However, in the final version of the show, certain details that spoke to instances of racial discrimination on the dance line were truncated or erased from the original interviews.

The final chapter examines *In the Heights* (2008) and *Hamilton: An American Musical* (2015), musicals that question how race affects immigration and national identity. *In the Heights* pointedly challenges stereotypes of Latinx characters as gang members and criminals and emphasizes the vitality of immigrant communities. *Hamilton*'s cross-racial casting insists upon the ability of actors of color to tell the story of the American Revolution. These musicals also question the terms of individual success and privilege inherent in the American Dream. For both the founding fathers pictured in *Hamilton* and the newest set of immigrants in *In the Heights*, race helps determine not only who might belong in America, but also what kind of lives Americans should aspire to.

Notes

1. Michael Omi and Howard Winant, *Racial Formation in the United States*, 3rd ed. (New York: Routledge, 2015), 12–13.

2. Stephen Quigley, "When Avenue Q Goes Local: Racism and the Production of Plays that Joke about Race," *Howlround*, September 25, 2015, https://howlround.com/when-avenue-q -goes-local.

3. Donatella Galella, "Feeling Yellow: Responding to Contemporary Yellowface in Musical Performance," *Journal of Dramatic Theory and Criticism*, vol. 32, no. 2 (Spring 2018): 67–77, 70, 67.

4. Website on "Principles for Building Anti-Racist Theater Systems," https://www.weseeyouwat.com/ (Accessed January 29, 2022).

5. Sarah Dahn, "White Actors and Directors Still Dominate Broadway Stage, Report Finds," *New York Times*, October 1, 2020, https://www.nytimes.com/2020/10/01/theater/new-york-theater-diversity-report.html.

6. David Savran, "Toward a Historiography of the Popular," *Theater Survey*, vol. 45, no. 2 (2004): 211–17, 215.

1
Racial Stereotypes, Major to Minor

The 2010 musical *The Scottsboro Boys* recalls how in 1931, nine African American teenagers were falsely accused of the rape of two white women and subsequently sentenced to death in Scottsboro, Alabama. John Kander and Fred Ebb frame this tragic history with musical numbers inspired by blackface minstrelsy. *The Guardian* describes the opening:

> The stage is barren save for a jumble of chairs. There's the tinkle of a band playing. Enter the cast: a white man dressed plantation-style, in a white linen suit and hat, two Black men in garish clown garb, and nine Black youths in the clothes of itinerant poverty. A sparkling, circus-style sign appears, reading "The Scottsboro Boys." A broad Southern voice announces that a tragic miscarriage of justice is about to be presented as a rollicking minstrel entertainment.[1]

Despite Kander and Ebb's intent to lampoon rather than to condone blackface, the Broadway production at the Lyceum

Theater was protested by those who called it a "racist play that has reduced the tragedy of the Scottsboro Boys case to a Step 'n Fetchit comedic, minstrel exhibition."[2] These protests prompted a carefully worded "explanatory insert" in the programs explaining to audience members that "*The Scottsboro Boys* uses the free-for-all atmosphere of the minstrel show to provide a fitting backdrop for the racially charged media and legal circuses that surrounded the real Scottsboro Boys trials."[3] But for protestors, the argument that *The Scottsboro Boys* was self-consciously ironic or provided a history lesson was an insufficient excuse for the pain of having blackface acting revived onstage.

Stereotypes reduce human qualities into an easily identified set of physical, linguistic, and behavioral attributes that predict a character's motivations and actions. Exaggerated, reductive, and often distorted, stereotypes encourage audiences to recognize characters immediately as endowed with special qualities or not worthy of attention. Such typecasting can arouse instant laughter or tears. It can also prompt concerns about ethical representation that make or break a production. As this chapter will detail, protests of *The Scottsboro Boys, Bloody Bloody Andrew Jackson* (2008) and *Miss Saigon* (1989) reveal frustration with the constant reenactment of racial types. Faced with these criticisms, white creative teams and producers respond that they did not intend to insult but were simply trying to do justice to an artistic classic, provide satiric humor, or use cross-racial performance in order to teach a lesson. Yet tensions over racial typecasting and impersonation continue to dog both revivals and newer productions.

Racial stereotypes comprised but some of the specific character types in standard use in American musical theater. Other kinds of typecasting, however, were less clearly defined by race. The villainous "heavy," the protective father, the dashing hero, and the attractive young ingenue were roles inherited from the classical and Italian *commedia dell'arte* traditions of earlier centuries. Racial distinctions became increasingly important in American theater throughout the nineteenth and twentieth centuries, as did the typecasting of national, religious, and ethnic groups such as in the roles of Jewish misers, drunken Irishmen, or belligerent German and Dutch immigrants. These characterizations were not just misguided theatrical fantasies. Though often comic in intent, they encouraged serious acts of marginalization and even violence. Blackface minstrel types, for instance, framed African Americans as naturally suited to slavery or service to white masters. St. Claire Drake has suggested that modern formations of racism developed to justify Black slavery as a worldwide system in which "the slave owner was expected to differ in physical type from the slave."[4] Used for both humor and dramatic intensity on the American musical stage, racial stereotypes serve as evidence of painful histories that include Native American genocide, slavery and Jim Crow segregation, US imperial expansion, and the xenophobic exclusion of Asian immigrants. This historical complexity is hidden under the stereotype's flat surface.

This chapter surveys three categories of racial typecasting, beginning with stereotypes originating in traditions of blackface performance. European opera and theater provided prototypes for the foolish Black slave and servant characters of the American stage. Premiering at London's Drury Lane in 1768, Isaac Bickerstaff's operatic afterpiece *The Padlock* featured a Black slave character, Mungo, who inspired both sympathy and laughter at his comic drunkenness. American performers of blackface minstrelsy later made singing and dancing blackface figures ubiquitous. White minstrels such as Thomas Dartmouth ("T.D.") Rice, who began his career as a traveling performer in the 1820s, made their fortunes performing song and dance in blackface. The Virginia Minstrels advertised their presentation of the "oddities, peculiarities, eccentricities, and comicalities of that Sable Genus of Humanity"[5] when they came to New York City in 1843. However grotesquely exaggerated, the characters played by Rice and other blackface minstrels were taken for accurate portrayals of Black character. For example, an 1840 description in a New York magazine praised what it saw to be Rice's presumably authentic portrayal of "Jim Crow."

> Entering the theater, we found it crammed from pit to dome, and the best representative of our American negro that we ever saw was stretching every mouth in the house to its utmost tension. Such a natural gait!—such a laugh!—and such a twitching-up of the arm and shoulder! It was the negro, par excellence. Long live JAMES CROW, Esquire![6]

Some blackface minstrel performances did promote sympathetic portrayals of Black character. Theatrical versions of Harriet Beecher Stowe's novel *Uncle Tom's Cabin* had iconic figures such as the elderly and long-suffering Uncle Tom, the brave mother Eliza, and the unruly Topsy.

However, these shows supported assumptions about racial inferiority, promoting nostalgic fantasies of plantation life in which Black slaves and servants loyally served white masters. Also popular were more disparaging comic portrayals of foolish and superstitious servants, fast-talking con men, or nubile "wenches," played by white men in burnt-cork makeup, reddened lips, and "woolly" wigs. In 1848 Frederick Douglass criticized white minstrels as "the filthy scum of white society, who have stolen from us a complexion denied to them by nature, in which to make money, and pander to the corrupt taste of their white fellow-citizens."[7]

Minstrelsy became immensely popular both internationally and across the United States, which helped to spread these racial fantasies broadly. Whether on Broadway or in amateur theaters, the cross-racial impersonations of blackface minstrelsy were everywhere, affecting how African Americans were seen both on and off the stage and upholding both slavery and "Jim Crow" segregation laws. These types remained a consistent part of American musical entertainment, sustaining a theatrical tradition by which white actors impersonated Black characters and maintained control over Black representation. As we shall see in the next chapter, sometimes "blacking up" was the only pathway to professional success even for African American performers.

Warriors, Savages, Princesses: Playing Indians

In 2010, *Bloody Bloody Andrew Jackson*, a rock musical depicting the populist appeal of Andrew Jackson, the seventh US president, opened at New York's Public Theater. The musical emphasized Jackson's relationship with his wife Rachel, and his part in the Indian Removal Act of 1830, which reneged on existing treaties with Native Americans and forced the abandonment of traditional homelands. Thousands of Cherokees and other Native Americans died on the "Trail of Tears" during their removal to "Indian Territory" in Oklahoma a thousand miles away. *Bloody Bloody Andrew Jackson* did not set out to glorify Jackson's actions, but satirized him as a kind of "American Hitler." However, critics of the show pointed out that it typecast Indian characters, and that despite the Public Theater's connections to the Native Theater Initiative and Native Theater Festival, the production involved little or no consultation with Native Americans. Navaho playwright Rhiana Yazzie, founder of the New Native Theater, commented on a 2014 touring production in Minneapolis. Yazzie decried on the problematic portrayal of Jackson as a modern-day emo rock star, who "will spew unchallenged racial epithets five times a week on soil that is still yet recovering from our own troubled history."

There is nothing about this history that is "all sexy pants," to quote the marketing machine that accompanied this show. The truth is that Andrew Jackson was not a rockstar and his campaign against tribal people known so briefly in American history textbooks as the "Indian Removal Act" is not a farcical backdrop to some emotive, brooding celebrity. Can you imagine a show wherein Hitler was portrayed as a justified, sexy rockstar? This play exacerbates the already deficient knowledge our country has when it comes to Native history; in that context, a false story about this country and our engagement with Native American people is unforgivable.

Bloody Bloody Andrew Jackson touched on the stereotypes of Indians that had been a part of American musical theater as early as *Tammany; or, The Indian Chief*, a heroic tragedy with music written in 1794 by Anne Julia Hatton. The depiction of Chief Tammany and his beloved Manana, who are ultimately burned to death in their cabin by villainous Spaniards, was a fantasy of Indian characters as barbarians, exotically beautiful princesses, and comic drunkards. Although the rest of the script has been lost, Hatton's song lyrics describe the image of an Indian hunter stalking deer in the woods ("Sure wing'd with death his arrow flies,/Then to his love he bears the prize") and then fighting in battle with a fierce "war-whoop."[8] A chorus of "happy Indians" immediately "laugh and dance and play" after the battle is over. In another song, an Indian character named "Wegaw" drunkenly declares that "deep sups" of liquor "have made foolish Wegaw quite wise" and imagines "Large lakes full of glorious rum!"

Whether pictured as fighting in battle or comically intoxicated, stage Indians were a popular feature on the nineteenth-century American stage in dramatic works such as John Augustus Stone's melodrama *Metamora; or, the Last of the Wampanoags* (1829). Fictional accounts of Amonute, a daughter of the Algonquian leader Powhatan who was given the nickname of Pocahontas, informed a melodramatic ballad-opera by James Nelson Barker, *The Indian Princess; or, La Belle Sauvage* (1808). While full of heroic battles and interracial romance, musical theater just as often used Indian characters for comic effect. John Brougham's *Po-ca-hon-tas; or, The Gentle Savage* (1855), included characters named "Kod-Liv-Royl," "Ip-pah-kak," and "Lum-Pa-Shuga" and Charles M. Walcot's *Hiawatha; or, Ardent Spirits and Laughing Water* (1856) included characters with the similarly ridiculous names of "Poohpoohmammi" and "No-go-miss."[9]

The US Naturalization Act of 1790 specified that naturalized citizenship would be granted only to the "free white person . . . of good character." Laws such as these ensured that Native Americans, persons of African descent, both free and enslaved, and Asian immigrants would be excluded from the rights and privileges possessed by American citizens. White settlers and their descendants sought to establish themselves as "natives" to the United States and other parts of North America, claiming authority over people as well as land, resources, and profits. As Philip Deloria has suggested, "playing Indian" has long provided a symbolic way not only to mock but also to appropriate Native identities; he notes how these performances "erased white acts of dispossession and generously mourned the fact that Indians were disappearing naturally."[10] Musical theater's representations of Indian characters could serve to justify colonial settlement, as shown in the 1924 musical *Rose-Marie*.

Set at a remote hotel in Fond du Lac, Saskatchewan, *Rose-Marie* features a love story between miner Jim Kenyon and French Canadian girl Rose-Marie La Flamme. Rose-Marie is being courted by the wealthy and urbane Edward Hawley. Edward hides his past affair with Wanda, a half-Indian woman, who continues to pursue him. In a climactic scene, Wanda stabs her current lover, the drunken and savage Blackeagle, and then pins the blame for Blackeagle's murder on Jim. By the second act, Rose-Marie has become engaged to Hawley, who promises her a life of luxury. But just as they are about to be married, Wanda dramatically stops the ceremony in order to confess to the murder. Realizing that she still loves Jim, Rose-Marie reunites with him in the picturesque setting of the Canadian woods. *Rose-Marie* offers several versions of "playing Indian," including white actors in redface playing the devious Wanda and the depraved Blackeagle and a stereotypically primitive ensemble dance number, "Totem Tom-Tom." A more subtle instance happens in Rose-Marie and Jim's famous song, the "Indian Love Call," a duet that includes a repetitive and modulating "Oooo" mimicking the imagined voice of the Indian lover. Through this monosyllabic refrain, the white lovers not only affirm their love but also insinuate that they have "gone Native" in the Saskatchewan frontier.

Stage Indians often function as either dangerous barbarians or noble savages who help white characters escape from the excesses of civilization and modernity. They also act as symbolic mentors for white characters, as does the character of Sitting Bull in *Annie Get Your Gun* (1946). In its light-hearted depiction of competing Wild West shows and the rivalry between sharpshooters Annie Oakley and Frank Butler, the musical includes a character based on the Hunkpapa Lakota leader. In real life, Sitting Bull appeared in Buffalo Bill Cody's Wild West shows and had a fond relationship with Oakley. However, the musical does not mention his significant acts of resistance against the US government, his participation in the Ghost Dance movement (Native American religious rituals that signaled potential rebellion), or his death at the hands of the police. Such details are extraneous to Sitting Bull's main function, which is to validate Annie through adopting her as an honorary member of his tribe. In the song "I'm an Indian Too," Annie imagines how "with my chief in his teepee./We'll raise an Indian family" and describes herself "looking like a flour sack/ With two papooses on my back/And three papooses on the way." She adds with a characteristic "whoop" that she imagines herself a "Sioux—ooh-ooh—a Sioux."[11] The character of Sitting Bull also functions to further Annie's romance with Frank. At the end of the show, he reminds Annie that she "can't get a man with a gun," convincing her to deliberately throw their shooting match and allow Frank to win. As with *Rose-Marie*, *Annie Get Your Gun* would not be complete without Indian characters who provide not only dramatic and comic effects but also validation for white characters. Indian stereotypes support the appropriation of Native cultures through redface impersonation and cultural imitation, and allow characters, actors, and audiences to "play Indian" in ways that further erase the presence and importance of Native Americans.

Curiosities and Perpetual Foreigners: Orientalism Onstage

Oriental stereotypes and settings were also popular in American musicals, presenting despotic rulers, exotic lovers, comic sidekicks, and spectacular scenes located in different parts of Asia, the Middle East, or North Africa. Many of these were inspired by European and British entertainments and operas. One influential work was Gilbert and Sullivan's 1885 *The Mikado*, a comic opera set in the fictional town of Titipu, which featured a trio of "three little maids" named Yum-Yum, Peep-Bo, and Pitti-Sing.[12] An even earlier influence is Molière's *Le Bourgeois Gentilhomme*, a 1670 comédie-ballet in which the social pretensions of the foolish Monsieur Jourdain lead him to promise his daughter to a "Turkish prince," who turns out to be a French suitor in disguise. American works such as Willard Spenser's 1886 operetta *The Little Tycoon* copied Molière's comic impressions of oriental royalty. A general who is infatuated with Japanese fashion has promised his daughter in marriage to the "Great Tycoon of Japan." The so-called Tycoon is, of course, not Japanese at all but American suitor Alvin in disguise. Alvin captivates the General with his fluent "Japanese," saying, "Yum yum boerum-jorum; ki-yi ki-yi! Sangar sangaree. Pongo-congo-ongo-wongo belladonna nux vomica, ki-yi." The General then gushes, "Pure Japanese! What a divine accent! What a glorious language! We shall all be speaking it yet."[13]

Other influences were less comic in nature. Giacomo Puccini's famous 1904 opera *Madama Butterfly* was based on David Belasco's 1900 stage play, itself a theatricalization of a 1898 short story by John Luther Long. Each of these works centers on the interracial romance between American naval officer Lieutenant Pinkerton and the young Japanese woman Cio-Cio-San. Cio-Cio-San is besotted by Pinkerton and devastated when he leaves her. She then learns that he has married a white American woman. In Long's story, she contemplates suicide but ultimately disappears along with her baby. However, Belasco and Puccini added a sensational death scene. The story's popularity led to multiple adaptations, each associated with different locations in Asia—Japan, China, the Philippines, and Vietnam. One successful version was Claude-Michel Schönberg and Alain Boublil's *Miss Saigon* (1989). Set during the Vietnam War, the heroine became Kim, a Vietnamese girl who has a relationship with an American G.I. Productions of *Miss Saigon* have been criticized both for yellowface casting and stereotypes of Asian femininity. *Miss Saigon*'s Broadway debut was protested by Actors Equity Association over the yellowface casting of Jonathan Pryce as the biracial Engineer. Three successive productions of the show staged in Minneapolis and St. Paul, Minnesota, in 1994, 1999, and 2013 inspired protests, including the website "Don't Buy Miss Saigon."[14] Commenting on a 2019 production in Madison, Wisconsin, Gwendolyn Rice notes *Miss Saigon*'s presentation of Vietnamese women as either "whores or victims" and its "white savior" narrative: "Kim puts all her love and faith into a white American who promises to save her from the chaos and danger of her own country."[15]

Other American musicals also combined exotic settings and cross-racial disguises with imperial power and interracial romance. *The Desert Song* (1926) is set deep in the Rif mountains of Morocco, where an Arab guerrilla unit, led by the masked "Red Shadow," is being surveyed by French Captain Paul Fontaine. Fontaine vows to capture Red Shadow and bring his head to his beloved Margot Bonvalet.

Unbeknownst to either Paul or Margot, the Red Shadow is actually a French soldier, Pierre Birabeau, who has created a secret alter ego in order to lead the Arab resisters. The show was inspired by the 1925 uprising against French colonialism by Moroccan fighters known as the Rifs. Yet the musical's emphasis is less on actual histories of colonial resistance than on romantic disguise and erotic tension. Pierre's cross-racial performance as the Red Shadow allows him to court his former flame Margot using oriental fantasies inspired by Rudolph Valentino in the film *The Sheik* (1921) and Douglas Fairbanks, Jr. in *The Thief of Baghdad* (1924). Disguised as the Red Shadow, Pierre sings "The Desert Song," describing "sand kissing a moonlit sky" and "a desert breeze whisp'ring a lullaby." While Margot strikes the Red Shadow across the face with her whip, she is nonetheless smitten by awakening passion. Both through Pierre's disguise and in the titillating role of Fontaine's lover, a Moroccan dancer named Azuri, cross-racial performance functions as a catalyst for the inner passions of *The Desert Song*'s white characters.

The more satirical *Anything Goes* (1934) incorporates oriental stereotypes and yellowface impersonation into a Depression-era farce. Billy Crocker and nightclub singer Reno Sweeney pursue Billy's newfound love interest, the heiress Hope Harcourt, onto a ship crossing the Atlantic for London. The ship's passengers include two Chinese characters, Ching and Ling, whose seemingly innocent demeanor masks their prowess at gambling. By the second act they are thrown into jail for having taken the money of other passengers. Wearing long hair in queues and speaking in unintelligible phrases, Ching and Ling resemble other stereotypes of

Chinese immigrants first arising in the nineteenth century. The figure of the "heathen Chinee," outwardly innocent and childlike but a cunning cheat at cards, notably appeared in Bret Harte and Mark Twain's 1877 *Ah Sin*, a play inspired by Harte's 1870 poem, "Plain Language from Truthful James, or the Heathen Chinee." These stereotypes registered the xenophobic fears of immigrants that led to a series of exclusion laws, beginning with the Chinese Exclusion Act of 1882, that barred Asian immigration and naturalization in the United States until after the Second World War. *Anything Goes* also echoes the familiar story of *Madama Butterfly* as Reno schemes to make advances to the British aristocrat Sir Evelyn Oakleigh in order to help break off his engagement to Hope. At first, the awkward and diffident Sir Evelyn is seen as a mismatch with the glamorous and worldly Reno. But it is revealed that years prior he had a "romp in the rice" with a young Chinese woman, Plum Blossom.

The oriental elements of *Anything Goes* are pointedly lightweight. Ching and Ling are not explored in depth even as their clothes, lost in a card game, provide a way for Billy and the gambler Moonface to disguise themselves and escape from the ship's jail. Likewise, the question of Plum Blossom is not explored deeply even as her story enables the musical's happy ending. Hoping to interrupt Hope and Sir Evelyn's wedding, Moon and Billy appear disguised as the parents of Plum Blossom. Reno then appears in Chinese costume as Plum Blossom herself. These disguises not only provide humor but also bolster confidence in the mutual attraction between Reno and Sir Evelyn. Thus these moments of typecasting and yellowface performance allow the marriage of

Reno and Sir Evelyn to circumvent presumably less satisfying motivations: Reno as a gold digger who pursues Sir Evelyn for his wealth or Sir Evelyn marrying Reno to disguise his lack of heterosexual desire. As in *The Desert Song*, encounters with oriental characters, whether literal or figurative, ensure the satisfactory closure of conventional forms of white romance.

Another type of oriental character appears in *Oklahoma!* (1943): a "Persian peddler," Ali Hakim, who complicates the courtship of the free-spirited Ado Annie by cowboy Will Parker. A traveling salesman with an exotic background, Hakim's worldiness contrasts with Will's naivete. Ado Annie is torn between her love for Will and her attraction to the "Persian kisses" of Hakim. Hakim functions mainly as a rival in the comic relationship between Will and Ado Annie, but he also appears in other scenes, including when the heroine Laurey deliberates between cowboy Curly and reclusive hired farmhand Jud. Throughout the musical, Hakim offers moments of erotic pleasure to the other characters: "Persian kisses" for Ado Annie, and pornographic pictures for Jud. Laurie also wants experiences outside of her plain life:

> Want a buckle made outa shiny silver to fasten onto my shoes! Want a dress with lace. . . . Want things I've heard of and never had before—a rubber-t'ard buggy, a cut-glass sugar bowl. Want things I cain't tell you about—not only things to look at and hold in your hands. Things to happen to you. Things so nice, if they ever did happen to you, yer heart ud quit beatin'. You'd fall down dead![16]

Hakim then sells Laurey an "Elixir of Egypt" that will put her into a deep sleep and elicit dreams of love and danger.

Whether in the form of kisses, objects, or elixirs, Ali Hakim provides access to the exotic, mysterious, and sensual realms that are conspicuously lacking in the more homespun lives of the characters. His role is based on the "Syrian peddler" in Lynn Riggs's 1931 play *Green Grow the Lilacs*, which inspired the musical. These ethnic designations suggest the actual presence of travelling salesmen and other merchants from the Middle East in Indian Territory (now Oklahoma) and other Western territories at the turn of the century.[17] This is referenced in the song "The Farmer and the Cowman": "And when this territory is a state/ And jines the union jist like all the others," then "The farmer, and cowman and the merchant/ Must all behave theirsel's and act like brothers."[18] However, the ethnic "merchant" is shown as someone who actively resists national incorporation. Hakim tries to flee marriage to Ado Annie, returning only after a shotgun marriage to another white female character, Gertie. Like the other outsider, Jud, he is not present to join the ensemble for the singing of the title song, "Oklahoma" which expresses collective celebration in the prospect of statehood and asserts white belonging and ownership over Indian Territory: "We know we belong to the land,/And the land we belong to is grand!"[19] It is the white settler, not the Persian immigrant, who is seen as the ideal American. But unlike poor Jud, Hakim nonetheless has a symbolic place in this community. Finally coerced into settling down, his new job running Gertie's father's store hints at a future that is consistent with his ethnic role—selling exotic adventures that go well beyond Kansas City.

Both in the past and today, theater has brought to life memorable characters that have influenced how real people are perceived and treated. Some racial types, like Ali Hakim in *Oklahoma!,* do not necessarily seem troubling or offensive. But others function in ways that go beyond light-hearted humor or entertaining spectacle. At its worst, racial typecasting reduces human beings to figures of subservience or exoticism and promotes ideologies of colonialism, slavery, xenophobia, and exploitation. But whether major or minor, stereotypes serve as reminders that much of American musical theater was created, performed, and revived by white artists and geared toward white audiences. However, as we will see in the next chapter, the history of Black musicals challenges this regime.

Notes

1. Candace Allen, "The Scottsboro Boys, A Minstrel Show Like No Other," *The Guardian*, October 29, 2013, https://www. theguardian.com/stage/2013/oct/29/scottsboro-boys-minstrel-show-accused-rape-new-york.

2. Kenneth Jones, "Protestors Take Aim at *Scottsboro Boys* Musical," *Playbill*, November 8, 2010, https://www.playbill. com/production/the-scottsboro-boys-lyceum-theater-vault-0000013656.

3. Jones, "Protestors," *Playbill.*

4. St. Claire Drake, *Black Folk Here and There: An Essay in History and Anthropology* (Los Angeles, CA: University of California Center for Afro-American Studies, 1991), 302.

5. Annemarie Bean, James V. Hatch, and Brooks McNamara, *Inside the Minstrel Mask: Readings in Nineteenth-Century Blackface Minstrelsy* (Hanover, NH: Wesleyan University Press, 1996), xi.

6. "Bowery Theater," *Knickerbocker: Or, New-York Monthly Magazine*, vol. 16 (July 1840): 84.

7. Frederick Douglass, "The Hutchinson Family—Hunkerism," *The North Star*, October 27, 1848.

8. These and the lyrics following appear in an edition of *The Songs of Tammany: Or, The Indian Chief* (1794) reproduced in James Henderson, "An Edition of the Poems of Ann of Swansea (Ann Julia Hatton, née Kemble, 1764–1838)," M.Ph. thesis, University of Glamorgan, 2005, 199–213.

9. John Brougham, *Po-ca-hon-tas; or, The Gentle Savage* (New York: Samuel French, 1898), https://hdl.handle.net/2027/mdp.39015021250298. Charles M. Walcot, *Hiawatha; or, Ardent Spirits and Laughing Water* (New York: Samuel French, 1856).

10. Philip J. Deloria, *Playing Indian* (New Haven, CT: Yale University Press, 1998), 51.

11. Irving Berlin, *The Complete Lyrics of Irving Berlin*, edited by Robert Kimball and Linda Emmet (New York: Knopf, 2001), 391–2.

12. See Josephine Lee, *The Japan of Pure Invention: Gilbert and Sullivan's The Mikado* (Minneapolis, MN: University of Minnesota Press, 2010).

13. Willard Spenser, *The Little Tycoon: A Comic Opera in Two Acts* (New York: William S. Gottsberger, 1882), 127.

14. Website, "Don't Buy Miss Saigon," http://www.dontbuymiss-saigon.com/.

15. Gwendolyn Rice, "The Heat is On in Saigon," *Isthmus*, April 3, 2019, https://web.archive.org/web/20191219201211/https://isthmus.com/arts/stage/the-heat-is-on-in-saigon/.

16. Richard Rodgers and Oscar Hammerstein II, *Six Plays by Rodgers and Hammerstein* (New York: Random House, 1959), 24.

17. According to the Oklahoma Historical Society, by the 1900 census, one hundred people identified as Syrians lived in Oklahoma and Indian Territories. The Oklahoma Historical Society, "A Fluid Frontier: Minority and Ethnic Groups and Opportunity in Oklahoma," https://web.archive.org/web /20201029004805/https://www.okhistory.org/learn/frontier4. For a more complete discussion of Aki Hakim and the figure of the Syrian peddler, see Charlotte Marie Albrecht, "Peddling an Arab American History: Race, Gender, and Sexuality in Early Syrian American Communities," Ph.D. dissertation, University of Minnesota, 2013, https://conservancy.umn.edu/ handle/11299/174848.

18. Rodgers and Hammerstein II, *Six Plays*, 54.

19. Rodgers and Hammerstein II, *Six Plays*, 76.

2
Beyond the Great White Way
Racial Progress and Black Musical Theater

After the 1980s, organizations such as Actors' Equity increasingly promoted "non-traditional casting" across the lines of race, gender, and disability. These principles were sometimes referred to as "color-blind casting," but in practice racial identity often made a significant impact on productions. For instance, in 1997 actress Whoopi Goldberg replaced Nathan Lane in role of Pseudolus in the Broadway revival of Stephen Sondheim, Burt Shevelove, and Larry Gelbart's 1962 musical, *A Funny Thing Happened on the Way to the Forum*. Having a Black woman play a slave character brought out a very different aspect of this leading role. Goldberg ad-libbed jokes about "Mammy" and her own interracial relationships, greeting an elderly white character with "What do I want to do with an old white man? I got one at home!" Goldberg's singing of "Free" also drew attention. In this song, Pseudolus imagines being "free to be whatever I want to be" and a citizen who is "equal with my countrymen." For Chip Crews in *The Washington Post*, the casting of a

Black actor made the connections between ancient Roman and US slavery too explicit:

> When a Black woman looks a blond man in the eye and says, as she later does, "I hate being a slave," we're suddenly, unavoidably light-years away from Roman farce, and "Forum" stops being "Forum." This material can't begin to support the resonances that have been unleashed. The house temperature seems to drop about 10 degrees, and the eerie chill lasts through her ensuing song, a now-disconcerting number called "Free."[1]

Read in another way, however, the song's newfound ability to provide an "eerie chill" can be seen as a much-needed update, as it did for Greg Evans in *Variety*. Evans noted Goldberg's "thoroughly modern style" and commented "this must be the first time "Forum" has been performed with dreadlocks." Evans saw this casting choice as "a welcome invitation to a new audience" who might otherwise "find this 1962 musical as dated as ancient Rome."[2]

Goldberg's cross-gender casting and improvised dialogue invited discomfort, but also demonstrated the power of a casting choice to change the impact of a revival. However, non-traditional casting alone does not necessarily alter how musical theater production has been tailored to suit predominately white audiences. Well into the twenty-first century, theatrical success continues to be defined in ways that maintain white perspectives and artistic dominance. Yet American musical theater has never been a solely white interest or enterprise.

This chapter surveys over a century of Black musicals, beginning with works written after the Civil War. While forgotten by many, these shows are nonetheless significant evidence of a long history of independent Black theatrical practice. Black theater companies began with the 1821 founding of the African Grove Theater in New York by William Alexander Brown and James Hewlett. The African Grove's repertoire included Shakespearean plays as well as original works such as Brown's 1823 *Drama of King Shotaway*. Its performances were produced primarily for Black patrons, a choice that prompted physical and verbal attacks from irate white people. Brown presumably responded to one such incident with a sign reading: "Whites Do Not Know How to Behave at Entertainments Designed for Ladies and Gentlemen of Colour."[3] Open only for a few years, the African Grove Theater was nonetheless the first of many efforts to allow Black actors not only to demonstrate and profit from their talents but also to perform in spaces free from white control. In 1926, W. E. B. Du Bois would describe the mission of the Krigwa Players, an all-Black theater company in Harlem:

The plays of a real Negro theater must be: 1. "about us." That is, they must have plays which reveal Negro life as it is. 2. "By us." That is, they must be written by Negro authors who understand from birth and continued association just what it means to be a Negro today. 3. "For us." That is, the theater must cater primarily to Negro audiences and be supported and sustained by their entertainment and approval. 4. "Near us." The theater must be in a Negro neighborhood near the mass of ordinary Negro peoples."[4]

Du Bois's vision has ever since served as a rallying cry for the formation of Black theaters and other organizations dedicated to artists of color.

Examples here begin with the musical play *Peculiar Sam, or The Underground Railroad* (1879), and then include the first Black musicals on Broadway, *A Trip to Coontown* (1898) and *Shuffle Along* (1921). Though different in style and content, these works raise common concerns about musical theater as a vehicle for racial advancement. Black upward mobility is similarly questioned in later Broadway productions such as *Dreamgirls* (1981), *Jelly's Last Jam* (1992), and *Bring in 'da Noise, Bring in 'da Funk* (1995), twentieth-century works that highlight Black creative artistry and affirm the importance of Black audiences seeing their own communities and histories represented on stage.

Crossover Hits: *Peculiar Sam* to *Darkest America*

Two of the most successful Black singers of the nineteenth century, sisters Anna Madah Hyers and Emma Louise Hyers performed opera, spirituals, and jubilee songs on the integrated concert stage and were featured in musical dramas. Their show *Out of Bondage* (1876) depicted a slave family in the south before and after the Civil War, with musical selections integrated loosely into the plot. *Out of Bondage* left a lasting impact on its Black audience members. Writer and singer Pauline Elizabeth Hopkins wrote, "for the first time, all the characters were represented by colored people," showing her the possibilities "for Negroes to appear in the legitimate drama."[5] Hopkins would go on to write musical dramas such as *The Aristocracy: A Musical Drama in Three Acts* (1877), performed by the Hyers sisters in 1891, as well as *Peculiar Sam, or The Underground Railroad*, written in 1879.

Like *Out of Bondage*, *Peculiar Sam* deals with an escape from slavery. Staged by the Hopkins Troubadours in 1879, the musical play revolves around the journey of Sam, his beloved Virginia, and other family and friends from Mississippi to Canada along the Underground Railroad.[6] Their path to freedom is threatened by their pursuit by Jim, a Black overseer who has forced Virginia into an engagement. Like many musical shows of the time, *Peculiar Sam* had a melodramatic plot punctuated with slapstick comedy, popular spirituals, minstrel tunes, and dances. Some of the characters were inspired by racial stereotypes, such as Sam's mother "Mammy" and his sister Juno, who resembles the rowdy character of Topsy from *Uncle Tom's Cabin*. At the same time, as Marvin McAllister suggests, *Peculiar Sam* subtly altered these "comforting, familiar moments of minstrelsy to subvert and complicate the entire performance tradition."[7] The virtuous and heroic protagonists Sam and Virginia are shown as capable of deep romantic feeling and familial loyalty. Hopkins recontextualized familiar spirituals such as "Steal Away" and blackface minstrel songs such as Stephen Foster's "My Old Kentucky Home" to emphasize the characters' powerful emotions as they escape slavery and travel to freedom. Hopkins's biographer Lois Brown suggests that *Peculiar Sam* "provided American audiences with the first staged reenactments of slavery that were not offered through the lens of the white imagination."[8]

Peculiar Sam gave its Black actors ample opportunity to show off their acting skills. Its title character (played by the popular actor Sam Lucas) performed multiple impersonations first as a *"gentleman overseer,"* then as Caesar, an elderly man, and finally a minstrel figure, "ole uncle Ned." At one point in the plot, Jim is fooled into thinking that Sam is a white man. These various imitations implied that Black people could successfully inhabit a range of social roles. At the end, the escaped slaves settle successfully in Ohio, and Sam becomes a US congressman. *Peculiar Sam* thus affirms emancipation, upward mobility, and political representation, illustrating how Black characters move from enslavement to model citizenry.

Similar demonstrations of Black racial progress would appear in other musical shows of the 1890s. Spectacles such as *Black America* (1895) and *Darkest America* (1895) also used minstrel stereotypes. *Black America*, for instance, was set in a "Negro Village" built in Brooklyn, New York, complete with log cabins, chickens, and bushes decorated with cotton balls. Advertised as having "500 genuinely southern negroes" brought "direct from the fields,"[9] the show featured minstrel numbers such as "Carry Me Back to Old Virginia," and "Old Black Joe," and showed its cast happily eating watermelons and dancing a cakewalk. At the same time, however, the show also included other representations of Black life. Advertisements described the second half as showing "the Afro-American in all his phases, from the simplicity of the southern field hand (especially the phenomenal melody of his voice) to his evolution as the northern aspirant of professional musical honors."[10] Though managed by a white director, Nate Salsbury, *Black America* was highly influenced by African American performer and director Billy McClain, whose 1894 play, *Before and After the War*, had similarly emphasized "The Progress of the Afro-American. From a Savage to Congress."[11]

In using stereotypes, these Black musical shows clearly emulated white minstrel companies, which were still in full swing in the 1890s. However, their large casts and successive scenes allowed for additional representations of Black character. *Black America* and *Darkest America* used plantation nostalgia and minstrel types as starting points to demonstrate racial progress from slavery to middle-class respectability. While the first act of *Darkest America* was billed as a plantation show, later acts were set on the levee at New Orleans at "the greatest steamboat race the world ever knew," and in "a home of luxury" in Washington, D.C., "sumptuously mounted with magnificent scenic effects."[12] The Black newspaper *The Colored American* praised the *Darkest America* cast as "half a hundred of the best Afro-American talent in the country," who are shown "carrying the race through all its historical phases from the plantation, into reconstruction days and finally painting our people as they are to-day, cultured and accomplished in social graces." [13]

"Our Own Shows": *A Trip to Coontown* to *Shuffle Along*

In the summer of 1898, *Clorindy—The Origin of the Cakewalk*, with music by Will Marion Cook and lyrics by Paul Lawrence

Dunbar, was performed on the rooftop garden of the Casino Theater, becoming the first Black musical show to appear on Broadway. Cook jubilantly described it as a major moment in Broadway history.

> When I entered the orchestra pit, there were only about fifty people on the roof. When we finished the opening chorus, the house was packed to suffocation . . . the show downstair in the Casino Theater was just letting out. The big audience heard those heavenly Negro voices and took to the elevators . . . . My chorus sang like Russians, dancing meanwhile like Negroes, and cakewalking like angels, Black angels! When the last note was sounded the audience stood and cheered for at least ten minutes. [14]

Cook declared that "Negroes are at last on Broadway, and here to stay!" Yet minstrel stereotypes still greatly inhibited Black creative success. James Weldon Johnson wrote that minstrelsy had "fixed the tradition of the Negro as only an irresponsible, happy-go-lucky, wide grinning, loud laughing, shuffling, banjo playing, singing, dancing sort of being."[15] Aspiring Black performers often had few professional options other than stereotypical characters and familiar "coon" songs, such as Ernest Hogan's notorious "All Coons Look Alike to Me." Despite his many Broadway successes, comedian Bert Williams still played familiar stereotypes using blackface makeup, telling interviewers that "I shuffle onto the stage, not as myself, but as a lazy, slow-going negro" and describing how "black face, run-down shoes and elbow-out make-up gives me a place to hide. The real Bert Williams is crouched deep down inside the coon who sings the songs and tells the stories."[16]

While many Black musical shows still expressed the hope of racial progress, this ideal was called into question. This skepticism is evident in *A Trip to Coontown* (1897), the first full-length musical comedy in New York to be entirely written, directed, performed, and managed by Black artists. *A Trip to Coontown* had its genesis in Robert Allen ("Bob") Cole's All-Star Stock Company, which formed in 1894. In 1896, Cole began working with the Black Patti Troubadours, a company formed around the success of soprano Sissieretta Jones. Billed as the "Black Patti" (a reference to the Italian opera singer Adelina Patti), Jones was the highest-paid Black performer of her time. One of the Black Patti Troubadours's original musical sketches was a "merry musical farce" titled "On Jolly Coon-ey Island," written by Cole and Billy Johnson in 1896, which later served as the inspiration for *A Trip to Coontown*.

Disillusioned by their experiences with Rudolf Voelckel and James Nolan, the white managers of the Black Patti Troubadours, Cole and Johnson left that company, taking their materials and some of the performers with them. Cole insisted: "We are going to have our own shows. We are going to write them ourselves, we are going to have our own stage managers, our own orchestra leader and our own manager out front to count up. No divided houses—our race must be seated from the boxes back."[17] Despite positive reviews in the fall of 1897, *A Trip to Coontown* faced obstacles, including a boycott organized by Voelckel and Nolan that made it impossible for the show to be produced except in third-rate

American and Canadian theaters. In the spring of 1898, New York booking agency Klaw and Erlanger finally broke the boycott and *A Trip to Coontown* opened at the Third Avenue Theater in New York City on April 4, 1898.

As suggested by its title, *A Trip to Coontown* included "coon" songs and stereotypes. The song "Chicken" details the adventures of Eph Jackson, a valet to a millionaire who, despite his exposure to a lavish lifestyle and world travel, clings to a crate of chickens that he brings wherever he goes. However, the musical also included a range of characters such as the hypocritical Reverend Sly and the long-winded Captain Fleetfoot, and Italian and Chinese caricatures played by actor Tom Brown. Like *Darkest America* and other Black revues, the second act of *A Trip to Coontown* featured displays of Black wealth in a grand reception with operatic entertainments set in the luxurious home of the elderly Silas Green. But the show also satirized the Black bourgeoisie, as two con men, Flimflammer and Willie Wayside try to swindle Green into investing in a fictional pleasure resort "Coontown." By poking fun at the newly rich Green, *A Trip to Coontown* indicated a degree of skepticism about Black racial progress.

An emphasis on Black communities and concerns would be taken up by subsequent musical comedies, including Broadway musicals featuring the popular team of Bert Williams and George Walker—*In Dahomey* (1903), *Abyssinia* (1906), and *Bandanna Land* (1908)—as well as Eubie Blake and Noble Sissle's hit *Shuffle Along* (1921). These Williams and Walker shows featured the humorous escapades of Black characters in spaces free from white presence.

In *In Duhomey* and *Abyssinia*, for instance, Williams and Walker played characters who travel to Africa in search of fortune. *Shuffle Along* is set in "Jimtown," a self-governing Black town that is about to elect a new mayor. The comedians Flournoy E. Miller and Aubrey Lyles, whose play, *The Mayor of Dixie*, was the inspiration for *Shuffle Along*, played political rivals Steve Jenkins and Sam Peck. A third mayoral candidate, the virtuous Harry Walton, is forbidden from marrying his beloved Jessie unless he wins the campaign. Harry and Jessie sing the tender "Love Will Find a Way," but the musical's most famous song was "I'm Just Wild About Harry," later chosen by Harry S. Truman for his 1948 presidential campaign. While aspects of *Shuffle Along* were quite formulaic, including blackface comedy by Miller and Lyles, it offered a versatile and talented cast as well as energetic ensemble numbers.

Shuffle Along helped to desegregate New York's commercial theater scene, with *Variety* noting with surprise on its opening night in May 1921 that "colored patrons were noticed as far front as the fifth row,"[18] a change from the segregated norm in which Black spectators were relegated to balcony seating. However, in December of the same year *Variety* commented that "the two races are rarely intermingled."[19] The Black newspaper *The Amsterdam News* reported that *Shuffle Along* enjoyed standing-room-only crowds "almost six deep."[20] The show launched the careers of African American performers such as Florence Mills, Fredi Washington, and Josephine Baker as well as inspired Langston Hughes to hail the show as a catalyst for the Harlem Renaissance.

Cautionary Tales: *Dreamgirls*

After *Shuffle Along*, Black performers continued to appear on Broadway in adaptations of operas and musicals such as *The Swing Mikado* and *The Hot Mikado* in 1939 and *Carmen Jones* in 1943, and in all-Black versions of *Hello Dolly!* (1967). Original Black musicals took the stage as well. Miki Grant's revue *Don't Bother Me, I Can't Cope* (1972) tackled issues of racism and feminism through jazz, funk, calypso, gospel, and rock numbers. Directed by Vinnette Carroll, it was the first Broadway musical with music, lyrics, book, and direction by Black women. *Your Arms Too Short to Box with God* (1976), based on the biblical Book of Matthew, was written by Vinnette Carroll with music and lyrics by Alex Bradford and additional songs by Miki Grant.

While late twentieth-century Black musicals had different themes, most often they revolved around the lives of famous Black musicians and entertainers. Examples include the tribute to Fats Waller and other Harlem Renaissance musicians *Ain't Misbehavin'* (1978), and the jukebox musical based on the Motown group The Temptations, *Ain't Too Proud* (2018). These musicals not only served as vehicles for popular songs but also commented on the challenges of Black performance. *Dreamgirls* (1981), written by the white creative team of Henry Krieger and Tom Eyen and inspired by legendary acts such as the Supremes and James Brown, followed in this vein.

At an amateur competition at Harlem's Apollo Theater, "The Dreamettes"—lead singer Effie White and her friends Deena Jones and Lorrell Robinson—meet Curtis Taylor, a car salesman who dreams of being a big-time manager.

Though they lose, Curtis gets them jobs as backup singers for rhythm and blues singer Jimmy "Thunder" Early, and ultimately helps transform them into a chart-topping group. *Dreamgirls* both celebrates these young Black female singers and shows the pitfalls of their success. Curtis convinces Jimmy and "The Dreams" that they should move beyond soul and R&B and instead record pop music. But Jimmy is unable to stomach Curtis's demands for crossover acts and is fired after inserting a wild funk number into one of his gigs. Effie is also deemed too unattractive to be the lead singer of a crossover group. Curtis promotes soprano Deena to lead singer and leaves Effie to marry her. The heartbroken Effie, who is pregnant with Curtis's child, is eventually replaced with another backup singer and the reconfigured "Deena Jones and the Dreams" then goes on to mainstream success.

Dreamgirls implicates Curtis's behavior in sacrificing Jimmy and Effie to pursue fame. After one of their recordings is plagiarized by white pop singers, Curtis resorts to bribery, paying radio disc jockeys to play their next single. This unethical action is framed as a survival tactic in a racist business. However, he later uses the same strategy in order to subvert Effie's recording of the ballad "One Night Only" and steal the song for Deena. The Dreams challenges the music industry's color line, but it is Curtis's self-centeredness rather than racism that stands out as the real problem. Effie's showstopping hit, "And I'm Telling You I'm Not Going," becomes as an anguished behind-the-scenes implication of Curtis's romantic betrayal rather than a means of calling out the industry's colorism and sexist beauty standards. While the 2006 film version of *Dreamgirls* inserted allusions to pivotal historical events such as the 1968 assassination of the Reverend Martin Luther King, Jr., such references were conspicuously absent from the stage musical. The libretto downplayed allusions to Black civil rights activism and radical liberation. Instead of being used as part of a rallying cry, as in Langston Hughes's poetic line, "What happens to a dream deferred?" or King's monumental "I have a dream" speech, the word "dream" ironically becomes identified with a marketing strategy through the signature song "We are Dreamgirls." Motivations become personal rather than political, as Curtis continually repeats to Deena that she is his "dream." Deena ultimately asserts her own independence in leaving Curtis and the Dreams to pursue individual success without the other singers. Yet the ending does suggest a degree of Black female solidarity as Deena and Effie reconcile and Effie joins the Dreams' farewell concert for a reprise of their signature song.

Echoing the real-life stories of Diana Ross and Florence Ballard, the musical repeats a familiar tale of musical success and backstage corruption that also appears in musicals about white performers such as *42nd Street* or *Jersey Boys*. But in *Dreamgirls* the racial significance of the crossover act adds an additional layer to this cautionary tale, insofar that commercial success inevitably entails Black cultural loss and betrayal. The Dreams can only rise to stardom by disavowing their connection to R&B, soul, and other Black musical forms. Deena's rise to solo fame is accomplished only by leaving Effie and the other Dreams behind. Even though *Dreamgirls* celebrates and showcases Black musical virtuosity, its story is far different from how earlier Black musicals envisioned Black racial progress in communal terms.

Connecting to the Black Past:
Musicals by George C. Wolfe

While it calls out instances of racism and sexism, *Dreamgirls* ultimately backs away from a deeper critique. A different story is told in *Jelly's Last Jam*, a 1992 musical written by George C. Wolfe, based on the life of the ragtime and jazz pianist Jelly Roll Morton (Ferdinand Joseph LaMothe, 1890–1941). Starting with Jelly's youth, in which he is banished from his mixed-race Creole family in New Orleans for playing piano in "sporting houses" (brothels), the musical emphasizes Jelly's rejection of his Black racial identity. Jelly performs Black musical forms but claims that "my ancestors came directly, directly from the shores of France. No coon stock in this Creole."[21] While the musical mocks Jelly's self-promoting claim to be the inventor of jazz, it does show him as an innovative composer and pianist. The otherworldly narrator, the "Chimney Man," describes him as "he who drinks from the vine of syncopation/But denies the black soil from which this rhythm was born."[22] Jelly's music is shown to be deeply rooted in the hybrid cultures of New Orleans, as he first encounters African, Caribbean, and Latin melodies and rhythms in the marketplaces of Congo Square. However, Jelly disavows Black influences and forces others into performing blackface "coon" numbers.

Jelly experiences a final moment of recognition before dying, singing "ain't no black notes in my song . . . I was wrong."[23] By foregrounding how Jelly comes to terms with his Black identity, *Jelly's Last Jam* makes a powerful statement about the need to prioritize racial connection and history over commercial success. History is made even more central in Wolfe's 1996 collaboration with Savion Glover, *Bring in 'da Noise, Bring in 'da Funk*. Using tap and other percussive forms of dance, opening scenes such as "The Circle Stomp" and "The Pan Handlers" depict the Middle Passage and slave life, suggesting how slaves, denied access to drums that might incite revolt, developed unique modes of musical improvisation and communication. Part two presents the terrors of the Jim Crow South and the Great Migration northwards with numbers such as "Lynching Blues" and "The Chicago Race Riot Rag," in which percussive tapping suggests the dangling feet of a lynched man or the repetitive sounds of factories. Later scenes depict the history of African American tap dance, paying tribute to "Master Juba," Bill T. Robinson, Harold Nicholas, and Fayard Nicholas. Inspired by dancer Savion Glover as "a living repository of rhythm," Wolfe describes that "these old black tap dancers, who were taught by the old black tap dancers" then "passed that information on to Savion, and it landed in his feet, and his being, and his soul."[24] This idea of history as transmitted through bodily movement is central to the musical: "With this show, we didn't want to bang people on the head with history but to explore what history truly is: an incredibly intimate phenomenon. History doesn't happen to cultures. It doesn't happen to races. It happens to people . . . When you fully claim your history, you can soar."[25] But though past and present are intimately connected, the show is skeptical of the myth of

Black racial progress. In sequences such as "Taxi," in which a Black businessman is successively ignored by cabdrivers, the musical emphasizes how professional status does not provide an escape from racism.

In 2016 Wolfe produced *Shuffle Along, or, the Making of the Musical Sensation of 1921*. Framing Sissle and Blake's score with backstories of *Shuffle Along*'s performers, Wolfe highlighted the contrast between lively numbers onstage and the difficult lives of artists behind the scenes. He celebrated *Shuffle Along*'s breakthrough success but also raised questions about its use of blackface minstrelsy, and how white composers such as George Gershwin appropriated Black music. In speaking of *Jelly's Last Jam*, Wolfe had criticized the dangers of Black musicals designed only for entertainment: "They've given you, you know, the gravy and a flash of grit so that you know there's some there 'cause it's sort of fun and dangerous but they really haven't gone inside. In telling the story of Jelly, the story of jazz, you gotta have grit to go with the gravy, you gotta have pain to go with the song."[26] In reviving *Shuffle Along*, Wolfe continues to "go inside" the lived experiences of Black performers and to connect the present and the past of Black musical theater in significant ways.

Notes

1. Chip Crews, "A Funny Thing Happened to 'Forum': Whoopi," *Washington Post*, March 7, 1997.

2. Greg Evans, "A Funny Thing Happened on the Way to the Forum," *Variety*, March 15, 1997.

3. Marvin McAllister, *White People Do Not Know How to Behave at Entertainments Designed for Ladies and Gentlemen of Colour: William Brown's African and American Theater* (Chapel Hill, NC: University of North Carolina Press, 2003), 2.

4. W. E. B. Du Bois, "'Krigwa Players Little Negro Theater.' The Story of a Little Theater Movement," *The Crisis*, vol. 32 (1926): 134–6, 134.

5. Pauline E. Hopkins, "Phenomenal Vocalists," in *Daughter of the Revolution: The Major Nonfiction Works of Pauline E. Hopkins*, edited by Ira Dworkin (New Brunswick: Rutgers University Press, 2007), 120.

6. Pauline E. Hopkins, "Peculiar Sam, or The Underground Railroad," in *The Roots of African American Drama: An Anthology of Early Plays, 1858–1938*, edited by Leo Hamalian and James V. Hatch (Detroit: Wayne State University Press, 1991), 100–23.

7. Marvin McAllister, "'Kno' You're Wally': Reinventing Slavery, Family, and Nation in Pauline Hopkins's Peculiar Sam, or The Underground Railroad," *Modern Drama*, vol. 62, no. 4 (Winter 2019): 391–421, 403.

8. Lois Brown, *Pauline Elizabeth Hopkins: Black Daughter of the Revolution* (Chapel Hill, NC: University of North Carolina Press, 2008), 117.

9. Bill Reed, *Hot From Harlem: Profiles in Classic African American Entertainment* (Los Angeles, CA: Cellar Door Press, 1998), 46.

10. Roger Allan Hall, "*Black America:* Nate Salsbury's Afro-American Exhibition," *Educational Theater Journal*, vol. 29, no. 1 (March 1977): 59.

11. Barbara L. Webb, "Authentic Possibilities: Plantation Performance of the 1890s," *Theater Journal*, vol. 56, no. 1 (March 2004): 77.

12. *Trenton Evening Times*, December 19, 1897.

13. *The Colored American*, November 4, 1896.

14. Will Marion Cook, "Clorindy, the Origin of the Cakewalk," in *Readings in Black American Music*, edited by Eileen Southern, 2nd ed. (New York: W.W. Norton & Co., 1983), 227–33.

15. James Weldon Johnson, *Black Manhattan* (1930; reprint, New York: Da Capo, 1991), 93.

16. Camille Forbes, "Dancing with 'Racial Feet': Bert Williams and the Performance of Blackness," *Theater Journal*, vol. 56, no. 4 (December 2004): 603–26, 623.

17. Quoted in William Foster, "Pioneers of the Stage: Memoirs of William Foster," *The Official Theatrical World of Colored Artists National Directory and Guide*, vol. 1, no. 1 (April 1928): 48–9, Black Culture Collection Reel, UCSD Geisel Library.

18. *Variety*, May 27, 1921.

19. *Variety*, December 9, 1921.

20. *Amsterdam News*, March 14, 1923.

21. George C. Wolfe, *Jelly's Last Jam*, lyrics by Susan Birkenhead, introduction by John Lahr (New York: Theatre Communications Group, 1993), 54.

22. Wolfe, *Jelly*, 4.

23. Wolfe, *Jelly*, 97.

24. Program notes for *Bring in 'da Noise, Bring in 'da Funk*, *Playbill*, vol. 96, no. 8 (August 1996): 23–4.

25. Program, *Bring in 'da Noise*, 23–4.

26. *Jammin': Jelly Roll Morton on Broadway*. PBS Great Performances series, 1992, https://www.youtube.com/watch?v=Yf-_mHCZmws

3
We Could Make Believe
Liberal Limitations and the American Musical

In a revealing moment in Stephen Sondheim's *Company* (1970), protagonist Bobby is asked by Marta, one of his girlfriends, "How many Puerto Ricans do you know? . . . How many blacks?" He replies, "Well, very few, actually. I seem to meet people only like myself."[1] Initially produced with an all-white cast, *Company* implicates Bobby's racial isolation as one of his many blind spots, a state of complacence that comes with his privileged yet unfulfilling life. But while some musicals pointedly sidestep the subject of race, others go out of their way to confront it. In *Hairspray* (2002), the white heroine Tracy Turnblad allies with Black students at her high school and helps integrate a popular 1960s television show. In *Wicked* (2003), Elphaba faces ostracism because of her green skin and struggles to protect animal characters from abuse, a story that implicitly comments on racial hierarchy.

These twenty-first-century musicals were certainly not the first by white creative teams to address racism. Over a half century earlier, Richard Rodgers and Oscar Hammerstein II's

South Pacific featured "You've Got to be Carefully Taught," sung by a white male character, Lieutenant Joe Cable, as he confronts his own reluctance to marry his Tonkinese (Vietnamese) lover Liat.

> You've got to be taught to hate and fear,
> You've got to be taught from year to year,
> It's got to be drummed in your dear little ear—
> You've got to be carefully taught! [2]

Cable laments fears "of people whose eyes are oddly made,/ And people whose skin is a different shade." His subsequent decision to return to Liat affirms the validity of interracial love. Moments such as these in *South Pacific* aroused criticism from Georgia legislators, who denounced the musical as an "offensive" justification of interracial marriage. State Representative David Jones said that "Intermarriage produces halfbreeds, and halfbreeds are not conducive to the higher type of society. We in the South are a proud and progressive people. Halfbreeds canot be proud . . . . In the South we have pure blood lines and we intend to keep it that way."[3]

This chapter looks in detail at *South Pacific* as well as two other twentieth-century musicals by white creative teams that challenged racial prejudice, Hammerstein and Jerome Kern's *Show Boat* (1927) and Rodgers and Hammerstein's *The King and I* (1951). These musicals not only made racial tolerance and interracial love stories central to their story lines but also provided sympathetic roles for characters of color and promoted more diverse casting practices. *South Pacific*, *The King and I*, and Rodgers, Hammerstein, and

Joseph Fields's *Flower Drum Song* (1958) drew from the semi-biographical accounts of James Michener, Anna Leonowens, and C. Y. Lee and promoted more liberal attitudes toward Asia, the Pacific Islands, and Chinese immigrants. However, despite their overt criticism of racial prejudice, these musicals reproduced some of the ways that American musical theater continued to give more weight to white characters and perspectives, and their initial productions featured blackface and yellowface casting. The chapter concludes by discussing how David Henry Hwang's 2002 revised libretto for *Flower Drum Song* reworked the 1958 musical's plot and further spotlighted Asian American performers, demonstrating how a musical might be radically reimagined even as its original songs and romantic love story are preserved.

Show Boat

Based on a 1926 novel by Edna Ferber, *Show Boat* integrated song, dance, and narrative, and was seen as a much more serious attempt at musical theater than the light comedies and revues of its time. The musical begins in 1887 with the Mississippi arrival of the Cotton Blossom, a showboat run by Captain Andy and Parthy Hawks, and centers on the love story between their daughter Magnolia and riverboat gambler Gaylord Ravenal. The first Broadway musical that allowed an integrated cast to perform together on the same stage, *Show Boat* made clear that its white and Black characters lived and worked in close proximity.

Show Boat highlights the tragedy of anti-miscegenation laws through the relationship between the Cotton Blossom's leading lady Julie La Verne and her husband Steve Baker. After Steve fights with the Cotton Blossom's engineer Pete for harassing his wife, Pete reveals to a sheriff that Julie's mother was Black. The sheriff, citing a Mississippi law prohibiting interracial marriage, threatens to arrest the couple. However, just before he arrives, Steve cuts Julie's hand and swallows some of her blood in order to declare that he has at least one drop of "black blood" in him as well. But even though they are saved from jail by this dramatic move, they are fired from the showboat.

As Todd Decker has pointed out, *Show Boat* not only featured Black soloists and chorus members but also emphasized Black musical performance as a vital part of American entertainment.[4] Even before the climatic reveal of Julie's passing as white, her mixed-race identity is suggested by her signature song, "Can't Help Lovin' Dat Man," earlier in Act I. The Cotton Blossom's cook Queenie is surprised that Julie knows that song as she has only heard "colored folks" sing it. That Magnolia later also finds professional success with this song linked to "colored folks" emphasizes how white entertainers often took on Black-inspired music and dance. In Act II, a struggling Magnolia, abandoned by Ravenal, auditions for a singing job at the Trocadero in Chicago. Julie, also abandoned by her husband Steve, overhears Magnolia singing "Can't Help Lovin' Dat Man" in preparation for her audition, and secretly quits her own job there so that Magnolia can take her place. Another memorable song in *Show Boat* gives voice to Black oppression when Joe, a dockworker, sings "Ol' Man River." Composed for Paul Robeson, the renowned actor who played Joe in the original London production, the song openly critiques how Black people "all work while the white folk play," and describes the "sweat and strain" of physical labor, "body all achin' and wracked with pain."[5]

However, *Show Boat* has been criticized for outdated language and reiterating blackface minstrelsy. Later productions have tried to update some of its more problematic aspects. For instance, a 1993 production in Toronto, directed by Hal Prince, excised an offensive musical sequence with "primitive gibberish lyrics,"[6] toned down aspects of Queenie's "mammy" role, and cast a Black rather than white performer in the "tragic mulatta" role of the light-skinned Julie.[7] This production received negative responses from community members as well as a cool reception from *Time* magazine's William A. Henry III, who commented that "The real problem is that the show follows the wrong story. It assumes that black people are inherently less interesting than whites."[8]

South Pacific

Set on an unidentified South Pacific island during the Second World War, *South Pacific* has two central romances. American nurse Nellie falls in love with an expatriate French plantation owner, Emile de Becque, but rejects his marriage proposal upon learning that he had previously fathered two children with a Polynesian woman. US Marine Lieutenant Joseph Cable visits the neighboring island, the mysterious

Bali Ha'i, and is introduced to Liat, a young Tonkinese woman, by her mother, an entrepreneur that the US Seabees call "Bloody Mary." Cable falls in love with Liat after their first sexual encounter, but wrestles with his prejudices. He departs on a dangerous spy mission, joined by Emile, who has been rejected by Nellie. Cable then dies in a Japanese military bombing. Nellie realizes the true depths of her love for Emile while consoling the grieving Liat, and at the end of the musical Nellie is shown waiting for Emile alongside his two biracial children.

These love stories reference the French and American colonization of the South Pacific and mark its legacy of racial and sexual exploitation. Even while strict rules prohibit dating between the nurses as commissioned officers and the enlisted men, Bali Ha'i is seen as a place of sexual recreation offering local women to military men. The musical dismisses this somber note through the light-hearted camaraderie of the Seabees and robust songs like "There Is Nothing Like a Dame" and "Honey Bun," sung by Nellie dressed as a Seabee and accompanied by the comical Luther Billis in a grass skirt and coconut-shell bra. French colonial presence is not singularly benign; after her initial rejection by Cable, Bloody Mary threatens to marry a terrified Liat off to an older French planter. Yet colonialism takes on a romantic rather than oppressive aura. While identified as a plantation owner who relies on Native labor and has had sexual relationships with local women, Emile is a genial presence—a loving father to his two mixed-race children and a gentle suitor who does not unduly pressure Nellie into marriage.

Histories of colonialism do not go wholly unnoticed in *South Pacific*. Both Bloody Mary and her daughter Liat are identified as Tonkinese rather than Polynesian characters. This designation allies them with Emile as French-speaking (Vietnam had been colonized as part of French Indochina since the late nineteenth century). However, Bloody Mary's cultural and racial distinctions from Native Polynesians are obliterated in favor of familiar typecasting. Her shrewd nature as well as repeated phrase "You like? You buy?" suggests stereotypes of Asian immigrants, as do stage directions describing her as *"small, yellow, with Oriental eyes."*[9] Bloody Mary's uncouth behavior also evokes anti-Black qualities of primitivism and savagery. Co-librettist Josh Logan recalled how African American actress Juanita Long Hall was selected for the role: "Only two roles seemed to give us trouble, Bloody Mary and Cable. But at an audition, a marvelous mulatto singer Juanita Hall with an Oriental cast of features took off her shoes and stockings and struck a squatting pose that said, 'I am Bloody Mary and don't you dare cast anyone else!'"[10] Juanita Long Hall's performance as Bloody Mary would go on to win a Tony Award, the first time this award was given to an African American performer. Notably, in early productions Black and Latina performers were consistently selected to play Bloody Mary, while the role of Liat was played in yellowface. Diosa Costello (a Puerto Rican actress, the first Latina on Broadway) played Bloody Mary in the second Broadway company of *South Pacific*, and according to Logan, was "the antithesis of Juanita Hall," saying that "whereas Juanita had a face of Aztec stone, Diosas was more like that of a frenetic witch doctor."[11]

Bloody Mary's "You like? You buy" becomes a chilling refrain signaling not just the selling of souvenirs, but also the offering of Liat to Cable. However, this troubling moment is quickly recast as a romantic encounter leading toward an arranged marriage. Richard Rodgers noted the resemblance of this story to that of Puccini's opera: "The more we talked about the plot, the more it dawned on us that onstage it would look like just another variation of *Madama Butterfly*."[12] Unlike Cio-Cio-San, Liat is portrayed as nearly silent, pantomiming her joy through Bloody Mary's song, "Happy Talk" rather than being featured through a song of her own. As presented in *South Pacific*, the Pacific Islands become playgrounds in which white characters can find pleasure and profit. As she tries to convince him to marry Liat, Bloody Mary tells Cable that her selling of grass skirts and shrunken heads will support his life of leisure: "You no have to work. I work for you . . . . All day long, you and Liat be together. Walk in woods, swim in sea, sing, dance, talk happy."[13]

Yet the islands are presented not only as hedonistic playgrounds but also as symbolic spaces of wartime heroism and youthful maturation. Interracial relationships with Polynesian and Vietnamese women affirm Emile and Cable's broadmindedness. Rejected by Nellie, who adheres to the prejudices of her childhood in rural Arkansas, Emile laments that even though he fled France for having killed a fascist "bully," he still faces intolerance in his new island home. Cable's song, "You've Got to Be Carefully Taught," links the wartime cross-cultural relationships of American military in Asia and the South Pacific to Black/white tensions in the

United States. As Christina Klein suggests, touting racial acceptance and other liberal values during the Cold War helped the United States demonstrate its moral superiority as a global superpower and multiracial democracy that deserved to triumph not only over Nazi Germany, but also the rising tide of communism in Asia and the Soviet Union.[14]

Cable and Nellie show themselves to be virtuous white Americans by overcoming their individual prejudices. But while *South Pacific* speaks out against segregation in the United States and fascism in Europe, it romanticizes imperialism and militarism in Asia and the South Pacific. Cable's death reverts to the conventionally tragic endings given to many interracial love stories. Nellie and Emile, on the other hand, have a much happier outcome. Emile's song "Some Enchanted Evening" emphasizes love as transcending the differences of age and background. Yet their eventual union is possible only because both Nellie and Emile are both white, and another dimension of racial order is subtly re-established in the final moments of the musical. Nellie rejects bigotry in favor of a new life in the Pacific Islands, but her happy ending looks forward not only to a multicultural family but also to the continuation of a colonial hierarchy. Nellie accepts her new roles as mother and teacher of Emile's mixed-race children, telling the children that they must mind her even as they teach her to sing "Dites-Moi" in French. In the ending tableau, Emile rejoins them at the head of the table, grasping Nellie's hand as a sign of their reconciliation. This ensures Nellie's future as the mistress of Emile's plantation, a position that presumably can only benefit from her newfound racial tolerance.

The King and I

The King and I was based on Margaret Landon's fictionalized novel *Anna and the King of Siam* (1944), which in turn drew from the memoirs of Anna Leonowens, governess to the children of King Mongkut of Siam (Thailand) in the early 1860s. Each of these works features a monarch whose tyrannical ways are seen as rooted in archaic traditions. Anna, a widowed British schoolteacher hired to teach Mongkut's many children, is presented as a civilizing force on the kingdom, where the many customs include polygamy and sexual slavery. Her enlightened modern principles and feminist independence are thus placed in contrast with a despotic oriental patriarchy. In spectacles such as the "March of the Royal Siamese Children," Mongkut's many wives and children are presented in ways that suggest the lascivious excesses of the harem. These spectacular scenes of polygamy further highlight the perception that Anna is needed as an educator. As such, her work helps further Western imperialism in Asia and the Pacific in a maternal and benevolent manner. Her song "Getting to Know You" establishes her warm relationship with her Thai students. While scenes of a white woman teaching civilized manners to Siamese children and their mothers might be unique to *The King and I*, similar images of white female teachers and their eager dark-skinned pupils were already common on the American stage in the children's "pickaninny" chorus in vaudeville and musicals. Jayna Brown notes that "In the United States after the Civil War, it was familiar practice for white women songstresses to take picaninny choruses with them on tour throughout the states," with the children playing the pupils of the singer-instructor, and the singer as "motherly schoolmistress."[15]

Anna teaches not only Thai children but also their mothers about the virtues of Western society and the relative insignificance of Siam on the world stage. In "Western People Funny," Lady Thiang and the chorus of Mongkut's wives sing of the ironies of "Western people" who make them wear a "funny skirt" and leather shoes that "bruise and pinch our little toes."[16] The song emphasizes how European women's fashion is "funny," but also suggests that the childlike Thai women are unable to fully grasp Western manners as they lift their cumbersome skirts and expose their bodies to a visiting British envoy. Anna is positioned as the white female rescuer and instructor of these Thai women and encourages Mongkut's new slave Tuptim to dream of escaping with her lover. Parallels are drawn between enslaved Africans in the United States and oppressed Thai women as Tuptim creates a dance sequence, "Small House of Uncle Thomas," based on Harriet Beecher Stowe's abolitionist novel, *Uncle Tom's Cabin*. Sadly, Tuptim and her lover are not allowed to escape Mongkut's despotism, but Anna's influence is clearly present when Mongkut finds himself unable to whip Tuptim. US slavery is thus paralleled with patriarchal despotism in Siam. But rather than linking Western colonizers with the African slave trade, the musical implies that Western colonialism serves only a benevolent purpose: to liberate oppressed and enslaved people from oriental despots such as Mongkut. The abhorrent practice of slavery is thus displaced from US history onto the foreign setting of Siam, and its continued practice implicitly justifies Siam's benevolent assimilation into Western ways.

Gayatri Chakravorty Spivak uses the phrase "white men saving brown women from brown men" to describe how British colonizers abolished the Indian practice of *sati*, the ritual burning of widows, in the nineteenth century.[17] Anna similarly works to save the Thai women from their own culture, presumably for their own good. She also effects a moral change on Mongkut himself, who although resistant, admits that Western acculturation is inevitable. Rodgers and Hammerstein end the story with his death and the accession of a new and much more modern king.

The original cast of *The King and I* had few Asian actors, none of them Thai. Yul Brynner, who claimed Buryat (Mongolian) in addition to Russian, Swiss, and German ancestry, became famous for playing King Mongkut. Richard Rodgers recalled his audition:

> They told us the name of the first man and out he came with a bald head and sat cross-legged on the stage. He had a guitar and he hit this guitar one whack and gave out with this unearthly yell and sang some heathenish sort of thing, and Oscar and I looked at each other and said, "Well, that's it!"[18]

Yet even though certain roles were typecast, *The King and I* did provide some new opportunities for Asian and Asian American performers on Broadway. One original Broadway cast member was dancer Yuriko Kuchiki, who performed Eliza in "Small House of Uncle Thomas."[19] Another was dancer and choreographer Michiko Iseri, who was featured in "Getting to Know You." Trained in traditional Japanese dance, and a member of a company that performed Chinese, Korean, Javanese, Balinese, Burmese, and Thai forms, Iseri was hired by choreographer Jerome Robbins as a consultant. She became frustrated by the choreography, later recalling that "I learned authentic dancing from the people that came from these places . . . I think it's a sacrilege to make the dancing like they're supposed to be 'Oriental.'"[20]

Esther Kim Lee has documented how in 1968 the "Oriental Actors of America," a group protesting yellowface and advocating for the "greater use of Oriental talents" joined with other organizations to picket *The King and I* for casting white actors in leading and understudy roles.[21] While their demands were not met, the group's efforts to draw attention to yellowface casting and oriental stereotypes set an important precedent for arts activism. In successive revivals on Broadway, *The King and I* became an active site of Asian and Asian American casting. The Thai children were often played by Asian Americans; Baayork Lee, a pioneering choreographer who created the role of Connie in *A Chorus Line*, appeared in the *King and I* at the age of five.[22] Groundbreaking Asian American directors and performers such as Tisa Chang and Nobuko Miyamoto had some of their earliest theatrical experiences in its productions. Despite these instances, yellowface acting continued to be used in *The King and I* for decades. In 1996, *Playbill* lauded Christopher Renshaw's revival as conveying a "feeling of authenticity and a respect for Thai culture" with additions such as an opening Thai prayer ceremony, adding that "For the first time all the Asian roles are filled by Asian actors."[23]

The details of Anna Leonowens's real life offer a more nuanced and diverse story than that which is told through *The King and I*. Born in Ahmednagar, India, Leonowens took pains to disguise her Anglo-Indian mixed-race heritage by claiming that she was Welsh. These biographical details suggest the intriguing possibility of revising the musical's libretto in order to do justice to these racial complexities. While no one has yet taken up this challenge, a more radical revision did happen for another Rodgers and Hammerstein musical when David Henry Hwang revised the book for *Flower Drum Song* at the Mark Taper Forum in Los Angeles in 2001 and then for Broadway in 2002.

Flower Drum Song

Even though they mainly featured white actors, *Show Boat*, *South Pacific*, and *The King and I* did allow Black and Asian performers new opportunities on Broadway. Rodgers and Hammerstein's 1958 musical *Flower Drum Song* took an even greater step in promoting racial visibility for Asian Americans on the musical stage. Inspired by C. Y. Lee's best-selling 1957 novel, *The Flower Drum Song*, the musical is set in San Francisco's Chinatown. Its story concerns an old-fashioned Chinese father, Master Wang, who sets up his eldest son Ta with a demure new immigrant, Mei Li. Mei Li originally came to the United States to marry Sammy Fong, a nightclub owner, but she immediately falls in love with Ta. Ta in turn initially prefers the Americanized and enticingly assertive Linda Low, a dancer who is already in a relationship with Sammy.

The original musical clearly pitched its characters and story to audiences familiar with Chinatown only from a tourist's point of view. The song "Grant Avenue" imagines Chinatown as located squarely in "California U.S.A." but with foreign attractions. Grant Avenue is a "western street with eastern manners," featuring shops in which "You can shop for precious jade/ Or teakwood tables or silk brocade" and restaurants offering "shark-fin soup," "bean cake fish," and even an exotic "girl who serves you all your food" who is "another tasty dish!"[24] But in addition to advertising the charms of exotic Chinatown purchases and waitresses to curious visitors, the musical celebrates a shift in American racial attitudes toward Asians and Asian Americans. With the liberalization of immigration laws after the Second World War, Asian immigrants were no longer completely shunned as undesirable aliens. Instead, they began to be seen as the "model minority," hard-working and loyal new citizens who could exemplify US racial harmony and global influence. The musical presented Chinese Americans as college-educated, well-to-do, and eager to adapt to American culture.[25] While Master Wang still clings to Chinese tradition, his family is thoroughly enamored of all things American, and both Sammy and Linda are thoroughly acculturated.

In "Chop Suey," Chinese American characters celebrate America as a multicultural democracy, singing that "living here is very much like chop suey." American culture is pictured as an amalgamation of things and places ("hula hoops and nuclear war,/Doctor Salk and Zsa Zsa Gabor" and "Boston, Austin, Wichita, and St. Louis") that is nonetheless unified in spirit: "something real and glowing grand" that "sheds a light all over the land."[26] But in its celebration of American life, the original *Flower Drum Song* downplays the significance of anti-Asian racism. While Mei Li's undocumented immigration is crucial to the plot, the musical makes light of the painful history of Chinese exclusion. In marked contrast with C. Y. Lee's novel, the musical's Chinese American characters do not express discontent with the United States. Their anxieties come from the presumed incompatibility of Chinese and American culture rather than from their racial marginalization.

David Henry Hwang's revision of Rodgers and Hammerstein's *Flower Drum Song* made drastic changes to this story, with Hwang commenting, "I wanted to write what Oscar Hammerstein might have wanted to write if he had been Chinese American."[27] His revised libretto preserves the romance between Mei Li and Ta but challenges the portrayal of Chinese Americans as the model minority and questions American assimilation. Rather than setting the play entirely in the United States, Hwang's libretto began with a glimpse of a rapidly changing China. Hwang's Mei-li is no longer a wide-eyed picture bride seeking love in a new country, but a refugee fleeing China after the persecution and death of her anti-Communist father during the Cultural Revolution. Hwang also emphasizes the prospect of a transnational identity in which becoming American does not mean forgoing Chinese culture. In the 1958 *Flower Drum Song*, Ta's romantic interests in Linda Low and Mei Li imply an incompatibility between American and Chinese identities. Ta calls his father "completely Chinese" and his brother San "completely American," finding himself trapped between these cultures: "But I am both, and sometimes the American half shocks the Oriental half, and sometimes the Oriental half keeps me from—showing a girl what is on my mind" (1959, 37). In contrast, Hwang's version of *Flower Drum Song* imagines a Chinese American identity that is fully hybrid. Mei-li tells Ta that "sometimes you seem a hundred percent Chinese. Then a moment later, you become a hundred percent American" but then tells him that he can be "a hundred percent both" (2003, 20).

Hwang questions the presumption that the United States offers equal degrees of freedom and opportunity for all immigrants. A chorus of immigrants at first declares, "My child will be born in America, and will grow up without fear, for she will know neither famine nor war," and "When I can do what I want, no man will ever be my master. When I can say what I wish, my lips will only speak the truth" (12–13). But by the second act they express disappointment in America, saying "Can someone take my child back to Hong Kong? I cannot make enough to support us both. I will send for him one day, I promise," and "I am a physicist! And they made me scrub floors, like a coolie!" (88).

Hwang's version of *Flower Drum Song* preserves the original score, including its campy nightclub acts. However, its perspective shifts away from a visitor's view of San Francisco's Chinatown to that of insiders forced to cater to tourists. "Grant Avenue" is now sung by Madame Liang, no longer imagined as a quaint and elderly aunt, but an aggressive entrepreneur seeking to transform Chinatown from ethnic ghetto to prime real estate: "We've got to show the Americans who we really are. No more inscrutable Orientals, but smiling all-American faces. Polite men, beautiful women, the finest cuisine in the world" (36). Master Wang and Ta are now impoverished artists, who must give up traditional Peking Opera to order to perform at "Club Chop Suey." The song "Chop Suey" becomes a glitzy show number with a female chorus parading around in giant, light-up take-out containers while a male chorus dances with giant chopsticks, prompting Ta to worry that the club has become "some kind of weird Oriental minstrel show" (72). Characters in the revised *Flower Drum Song* still perform oriental stereotypes, but only because they must please predominately white audiences.

However, Hwang shifts the gaze to highlight how Asian Americans perform for one another as well. The 1958 *Flower Drum Song* was the first Broadway musical with nearly all performers of Asian descent, a casting feat that would not be repeated until Stephen Sondheim's *Pacific Overtures* in 1976. Hwang describes being inspired by the film, calling it a "kind of a guilty pleasure" insofar that it was "one of the only big Hollywood films where you could see a lot of really good Asian actors onscreen, singing and dancing and cracking jokes."[28] Hwang emphasizes how the value of *Flower Drum Song* lies not only in its association with Rodgers and Hammerstein but also in the performances of Asian and Asian American actors that would inspire later theater artists. His revised ending has Mei-li and Ta starting their own theater company in order "to tell new stories—of life in America" (96). This announcement is followed by a metatheatrical moment in which cast members speak directly to the audience and state their actual places of birth.

With this final celebration of actors of Asian descent, Hwang's *Flower Drum Song* gives a nod to Asian American theater companies such as Los Angeles's East West Players, founded in 1965. EWP seasons have included productions of *A Chorus Line*, *Cabaret*, *Little Shop of Horrors*, and *Sweeney Todd*, as well as works by Asian American creative teams such as *Beijing Spring* (1999) and *Imelda* (2005), and *Allegiance* (2012). The Twin Cities-based company Theater Mu has helped develop original musicals such as *The Walleye Kid* (2005) and *Half the Sky* (2019). Unsurprisingly, David Henry Hwang's version of *Flower Drum Song* has been produced by these companies as well. As played for Asian American spectators, this new *Flower Drum Song* becomes much more than yet another revival of the Rodgers and Hammerstein oeuvre. It highlights the value not only of allowing Asian and Asian American performers to take center stage but also of purposefully reinventing the roles in which they appear.

Notes

1. George Furth, Stephen Sondheim, and Hal Prince, *Company: A Musical Comedy* (New York: Random House, 1970), 60.

2. Richard Rodgers and Oscar Hammerstein II, *Six Plays by Rodgers and Hammerstein* (New York: Random House, 1959), 346.

3. "Georgia Legislators Score 'South Pacific'; see Red Philosophy in Song Against Bias," *New York Times*, March 1, 1953.

4. Todd Decker, *Show Boat: Performing Race in an American Musical* (New York: Oxford University Press, 2013).

5. Jules Bledsoe played the role of Joe in the Broadway premiere in 1927.

6. Robin Breon, "Show Boat: The Revival, the Racism," *TDR*, vol. 39, no. 2 (Summer 1995): 86–105.

7. Julie was played by Lonette McKee, the first African American to play this role.

8. William A. Henry III, "Rough Sailing for a New *Show Boat*," *Time*, November 1, 1993, 77.

9. Rodgers and Hammerstein II, *Six Plays*, 282.

10. Joshua Logan, *Josh: My Up and Down, In and Out Life* (New York: Delacorte Press, 1976), 283.

11. Logan, *Josh*, 244.

12. Richard Rodgers, *Musical Stages: An Autobiography* (New York: Da Capo, 1995), 259.

13. Rodgers and Hammerstein II, *Six Plays*, 337.

14. Christina Klein, *Cold War Orientalism: Asia in the Middlebrow Imagination, 1945–1961* (Berkeley, CA: University of California Press, 2003).

15. Jayna Brown, *Babylon Girls: Black Women Performers and the Shaping of the Modern* (Durham, NC: Duke University Press, 2008), 50.

16. Rodgers and Hammerstein II, *Six Plays*, 414.

17. Gayatri Spivak, "Can the Subaltern Speak? Speculations on Widow Sacrifice," *Wedge*, vol. 7–8 (Winter–Spring 1985): 120–30.

18. Richard Rodgers, interview with Arnold Michaelis, December 18, 1957, quoted in Frederick Nolan, *The Sound of Their Music: The Story of Rodgers and Hammerstein* (New York: Walker and Company 1978), 170.

19. Henry Gerrit, "That Cute Eliza in 'The King and I' Runs the Whole Show Now," *People Magazine*, May 2, 1977, http://people.com/archive/that-cute-eliza-in-the-king-and-i-runs-the-whole-show-now-vol-7-no-17/.

20. Hana C. Maruyama, "Getting to Know You: Broadway Meets Heart Mountain," *Asian American Writers Workshop Magazine*, October 15, 2015, http://aaww.org/michiko-iseri-heart-mountain/.

21. Esther Kim Lee, *A History of Asian American Theater* (Cambridge: Cambridge University Press, 2006), 29–30.

22. Sylviane Gold, "On Broadway: Revising Robbins," *Dance Magazine*, March 1, 2015, https://www.dancemagazine.com/on-broadway-revising-robbins-2306957611.html.

23. Sheryl Flatow, "Rediscovering the King," *Playbill*, vol. 96, no. 8 (August 1996): 12–16, 14.

24. Richard Rodgers, Oscar Hammerstein II, and Joseph Fields, *Flower Drum Song* (New York, Farrar, Straus, and Cudahy, 1959), 78.

25. Heidi Kim, *Illegal Immigrants/Model Minorities: The Cold War of Chinese American Narrative* (Philadelphia, PA: Temple University Press, 2020).

26. "Chop Suey," in *Flower Drum Song*, edited by Richard Rodgers, Oscar Hammerstein II, and Joseph Fields (New York, Farrar, Straus, and Cudahy, 1959), 61–3.

27. Quoted in Karen Wada, "Afterword to *Flower Drum Song*," with book by David Henry Hwang (New York: Theater Communications Group, 2003), 100. Subsequent page numbers appear parenthetically.

28. Misha Berson, "A Drum with a Difference," *American Theater*, February 2002, 14–18, 76.

4
Dance Ten, Looks Three
The Chorus Line and the Color Line

In one of *Flower Drum Song*'s nightclub routines, a Chinese American "vagabond sailor" sings about the different "girls who adored me" and now are "gliding through my memoree."[1] As he recalls these past encounters, Asian female chorus members parade around him dressed in different costumes, including a "stately Scandinavian type,/A buxom, blue-eyed blonde," and a "dancing chick" from "sunny Barcelona" playing castanets. Stage directions read "*The girls he refers to in the following refrain enter one by one, on cue, from the upper arches. In spite of his descriptions they are all undeniably Asian.*" The humor of this moment relies on the presumption that the Asian chorus girl is unable to pass as a British or European woman because of her appearance—and, in one case, her accent:

> **Frankie**   A sweet colleen from Ireland,
> Her hair was fiery red,
> Her eyes gave out a green light
> That said I could go ahead.
> (*Holding a microphone before her mouth*)

Say something Irish.
"Irish" Girl   Ellin go blah.

The discrepancy between the *"undeniably Asian"* attributes of these chorus members and the roles they play identifies a basic assumption: that the American chorus girl should be white. Like so many other white actors before her, the white showgirl can presumably embody a host of different ethnic and national identities, whereas the "Chinese" chorine remains an endearingly deficient copy of a white character.

How did whiteness become the default for the American chorus line? These racial conventions for casting were clearly shaped by the nineteenth-century transatlantic circulation of musical theater. American chorus lines evolved from the ensembles of earlier British and European dance and music: the corps de ballet, opera choruses, and the dance lines of burlesque and music hall. For instance, the influential melodramatic comedy *The Black Crook* (1866) featured among its many acts a troupe of French ballet dancers and a marching chorus of "Amazons." Elaborate spectacles of women in tights and other risqué costumes appeared in burlesque shows, first made popular in the United States by the 1868 tour of Lydia Thomson and Pauline Markham and their troupe of "British Blondes." Other British influences on American chorus lines included the "Tiller Girls," young women trained in toe dancing, kick lines, tap, and marching routines through John Tiller's London and Manchester schools, starting in the 1890s. There were also the fashionable "Gaiety Girls" who posed demurely in the 1880s shows of George Edwardes at the Gaiety Theater in London.

Derek and Julia Parker describe how the Gaiety Girl "sat (beautifully) while the star did a number—perhaps moving an elegant arm in time to the music, pointing a neat foot in one direction, then another, and walking sinuously around the stage. Nothing very demanding; nothing requiring years of training, concentration, pain."[2]

Whether dancing vigorously or simply walking and standing, whether clad in sophisticated fashion or gaudy costume, chorus lines were known for their displays of the feminine body. The female chorus was made even more popular by Florenz Ziegfeld, Jr., whose *Follies* began in 1907 and were produced each year until 1931. Inspired by Paris's Folies Bergére, with its extravagant stage designs and costumes, comedy sketches, song and dance numbers, and artful displays of female nudity, these musical revues featured numerous women in lavish spectacles performing intricately choreographed routines to the music of Irving Berlin, George Gershwin, Jerome Kern, Victor Herbert, and other prominent composers. Known as "Ziegfeld Girls," these chorines became popular models for white feminine beauty, style, and attractiveness.

Displays of white feminine beauty on the chorus line were informed by racial ideologies that influenced government policies and standards of fitness, health, and beauty. From the 1880s on, the American eugenics movement lobbied for the sterilization of those deemed unfit for American society, including poor, disabled, and mentally ill women as well as women of color. Race continued to inform the criteria by which people were judged as ideal Americans, with widespread beliefs about the genetic superiority of Nordic,

Germanic, and Anglo-Saxon peoples leading to the legal exclusion of immigrants from Asia, Africa, and Central and South America as well as restrictions on immigrants from Southern and Eastern Europe.

Even while these chorus lines emphasized white feminine perfection, their lavish spectacles were enhanced by performances of Otherness. A chorus of Indian "squaws" had appeared as early as 1856 in the musical extravaganza *Hiawatha*. Reviewing R. H. Burnside and Manuel Klein's *A Trip to Japan* (1909), *The New York Times* describes how chorus members were expected to switch rapidly from one familiar racial type to another.

> It is in the first of these scenes that a clever negro song and dance is introduced, in which so many chorus girls take part that it is impossible to count them, all apparently blacked up. It is heartrending to feel that they would be compelled to get their faces clean in time to be Japanese ladies in the ensuing scene.[3]

These cross-racial performances provided additional novelty, interest, and sex appeal to chorus numbers. David Roediger has observed that "genius" for white minstrels in blackface was "to be able to both display and reject the 'natural self,' to be able to take on blackness convincingly and to take off blackness convincingly."[4] Chorus lines followed a similar logic, using racial impersonation in ways that affirmed the whiteness of the performers.

Well before the successes of his *Follies*, Florenz Ziegfeld experimented with striking chorus numbers based on racial typecasting. In 1898, Ziegfeld and William A. Brady staged

A Guy Deceiver, which included Chester Bailey Fernald's *The Cat and the Cherub*, a one-act play "about Chinese life in San Francisco," and a performance by Ziegfeld's first wife, Anna Held. Held's featured number included an enormous "animated song sheet," which was used as her backdrop. According to a biography of Ziegfeld, while she sang, "the heads of Black singers popped up one at a time from the black notes on the song's score; at each chorus the heads appeared simultaneously and accompanied Held."[5] While the Ziegfeld Girls came from different cultural backgrounds, their ethnic differences were eclipsed by a professional image of white feminine beauty that was staged in contrast with Black, oriental, and Indian characterizations. As Linda Mizejewski has commented, the female soloists and chorus members of Ziegfeld's shows often served as "an enclave of whiteness within a far more racially and ethnically mixed montage of images and stereotypes."[6] The *Follies of 1907* included "a reincarnated Captain John Smith and Pocahontas visiting New York,"[7] and The *Follies of 1913* had a prologue delivered by "Chief Hawkeye" as he and "his Indian friends looked down upon night life in New York City."[8] Blackface minstrel comedy was used frequently, as were oriental numbers depicting opium dens and harems. The Ziegfeld chorines appeared as harem slave girls in "The Palace of Beauty" (1912) and "The Treasures of the East" (1926) and in blackface as the "Follies Pickaninnies" (1919).[9] The 1919 *Follies* featured a minstrel number with white comedians Eddie Cantor and George Le Maire joined by Bert Williams, all appearing in blackface. The show then continued with a choreographed pantomime by Maurice Mouvet and Florence Walton, with Mouvet playing a dangerous "Chinaman" who had "designs on Miss Walton who, in a drug-induced trance, danced almost nude."[10]

Specialty acts in the *Ziegfeld Follies* included notable performers such as Williams, Fanny Brice, and Will Rogers, who provided racial and ethnic diversity to comic routines. At the same time, the *Follies* remained most famous for its white showgirls, many of whom were valued mainly for their appearance. While some of the Ziegfeld numbers required considerable dancing or athletic ability, others did not. One popular number was the fashion show in which a procession of showgirls in different gowns slowly walked down runways and staircases. A former Ziegfeld chorus member, Doris Eaton Travis, remarked that "the showgirls were young, tall, beautiful, and wonderfully costumed and were required only to walk with elegance and grace."[11] The *Follies* further differentiated between the dance line and the chorus showgirl with movements that distinguished "the dancers from the parading clothes model/showgirls."[12] Beginning in 1922, Ziegfeld advertised the *Follies* as "A National Institution—Glorifying the American Girl."[13] This image of the white chorus girl as the paragon of American feminine beauty was promoted not only in the theater but also by popular Depression-era films directed by Busby Berkeley. In movies such as *42nd* Street (1933), *Footlight Parade* (1933), *Dames* (1934), and *Gold Digger* series (1933, 1935, and 1937), women in the chorus line continued to act as symbols of American class mobility, holding out the possibilities of glamour, fame, and fortune through musical theater.

Black and Oriental in the Chorus Line

Through popular shows such as Ziegfeld's *Follies*, the presentation of seemingly uniform white female bodies moving in unison became a standard part of the American musical. But white women were not the only ones to appear in chorus lines. Sam T. Jack's *Creole Burlesque Show* ran in theaters in Boston, New York, Chicago, and elsewhere between 1890 and 1897. It featured numerous female stars performing in dramatic sketches and variety acts, but its greatest appeal was a chorus of sixteen light-skinned teenaged chorus girls. In his book *Black Manhattan* (1930), James Weldon Johnson would riff on Ziegfeld's claim that the *Follies* glorified the American Girl in remembering "a Negro show different from anything yet thought of, a show that would glorify the colored girl."[14] *The Creole Show* presented these chorines not only as glamorous and attractive as Black women but also as able to play other racial types. The showgirls were described not only as "Enchantresses of the Mississippi" but also as "Charmers of the Nile."[15]

The Creole Show ushered in a new version of the chorus line, one that provided Black women with new opportunities. Once exclusively white, burlesque houses and other theatrical venues began to hire Black women. Jayna Brown describes how, for Black female dancers in particular, "stage performance was an alternative to the bedroom work of sexual labor offered by the sex trade as well as to the backbreaking and poorly paid scullery and laundry work in middle-class households. It offered Black working-class women mobility and independence. They could earn a good living expressing themselves creatively, working alongside friends and lovers."[16]

The Creole Show allowed Black women not only to break into show business but also to challenge all-white standards of female talent, beauty, and sex appeal. John T. Isham, the Black manager for *The Creole Show*, displayed Black female chorus lines in his own shows *Isham's Octoroons* (1895) and *Oriental America* (1896). Black musicals as well as nightclub acts began to employ Black female dancers. However, there remained troubling aspects of this new interest. Colorism remained a factor in these shows, with explicit preference given to lighter-skinned women based on systems of white racism that, as Brenda Dixon Gottschild points out, "valued white womanhood above all else and recognized beauty only in imitation of that standard."[17] The popularity of the Black chorus line did not mean that the women employed in them were highly paid or thought respectable. Black female bodies had long been exploited as objects of sexual desire. According to Irving Ziedman, what began as the more restrained "leg shows" of American burlesque—extravagant musical numbers with dancing chorines in revealing silk tights—later featured increasingly more explicit "cootch" numbers: "Blondes were supplanted by the vogue of "Oriental" dancers, Little Egypt was followed by Little Africa."[18] While white women performing on the chorus line sometimes benefited by becoming celebrities and marrying wealthy admirers, there were far fewer success stories for Black chorus members. With the exception of Josephine Baker, who rose to fame after moving to Paris, the spotlight continued to shine mainly on the white chorus girl.

Newspaper accounts suggest that there was disproportionate pressure on Black dancers to show extraordinary physical skill and endurance. If the white Ziegfeld Girl could be admired simply for her posing, Black female chorines were judged mainly for their dance moves. Part of the great success of *Shuffle Along* in 1921 was without a doubt its dance sequences. The show featured three female choruses—the Jazz Jasmines, the Happy Honeysuckles, and the Majestic Magnolias—as well as a male chorus, the Syncopating Sunflowers, all elaborately costumed. Photographs show the female chorines in various costumes: "cotton picker" overalls with straw hats, dapper top hats and shiny one-piece outfits, elaborately draped satin gowns, and even a set of what Eubie Blake described as "vaguely Orientalish costumes."[19] The choreography of *Shuffle Along* demanded that the chorus members demonstrate not only speed and precision but also the ability to shift between many different dance styles. For instance, the song "I'm Just Simply Full of Jazz," mentions the exotic "Salome" dance, Hawaiian hula, and popular Black dances such as "Ball the Jack" and the "Shimmie."[20] The *New York Herald* wrote:

> It is when the chorus and principals of a company that is said to contain the best negro troupers in these parts gets going in the dances that the world seems a brighter place to live in. They wriggle and shimmy in a fashion to outdo a congress of eels, and they fling their limbs about without stopping to make sure that they are securely fastened on.[21]

The *Chicago Herald Examiner* noted: "Every chorister dances like a demon and together they move with precision and lightness."[22]

The superlative skills of Black chorus dancers were apparent in other shows as well. One reviewer stated that the dance lines of Perry Bradford and Spencer Williams's Black musical revue *Put and Take* (1921) surpassed any "chorus of white girls on Broadway this season or for many seasons past."[23] Another said: "After viewing the blasé slouch of our many of our Broadway queens, it is a relief to see . . . real snap and verve."[24] After seeing J. Leubrie Hill's Black revue *Darktown Follies* playing in Harlem's Lafayette Theater in 1913, Ziegfeld bought the rights to several songs and dances for his own *Follies* in August 1914.[25] He hired Ethel Williams from the chorus line in *Darktown Follies* to teach the dances to his white chorus members. However, Ziegfeld did not hire any Black chorus members, nor did he mention J. Leubrie Hill in his program.[26] Furthermore, the 1922 edition of the *Ziegfeld Follies* parodied successful Black shows in a number sung by Gilda Gray, "It's Getting Dark on Old Broadway."

You see the change in ev'ry cabaret
It's just like an eclipse on the moon,
Ev'ry cafe now has the dancing coon.
Pretty choc'late babies
Shake and shimmie ev'rywhere
Real darktown entertainers hold the stage,
You must black up to be the latest rage.
Yes, the great white way is white no more,
It's just like a street on the Swanee shore;
It's getting very dark on old Broadway.[27]

For this number, the white women of Ziegfeld's chorus wore white costumes and hats that glowed in the dark and the stage lights were turned down to darken their faces.[28]

A Chorus Line

While "It's Getting Dark on Old Broadway" suggested white envy over the popularity of Black chorus dancers, the real lives of Black chorines remained full of professional and personal challenges. In her book *Wayward Lives, Beautiful Experiments*, Saidiya Hartman considers the career of Mabel Hampton, a dancer who appeared in *Come Along, Mandy* and *Blackbirds of 1926*. Hartman imagines a complex and passionate interior life for Mabel:

> At the music hall, cabaret, and private party, Mabel tried to dance her way into feeling free, to compose a wild and beautiful life, to step onto an errant path that might guide her to the wonderful experiences afforded by Harlem. Every step executed on the dance floor was an effort to elude the prohibitions and punishments that increasingly hemmed in the ghetto and that awaited young women daring to live outside the boundaries of marriage and servitude or move through the city unescorted by a husband or brother.[29]

Hartman's eloquent account emphasizes how the synchronized, harmonious movement of the chorus line belied the real struggles faced by dancers, especially Black women. It also underscores how dance functions both as a means of self-expression and as employment.

The 1975 Broadway hit *A Chorus Line* makes a similar contrast between the uniform perfection of the chorus line and the struggles of individual dancers, albeit in ways that both highlight and obscure racial disparities. Set on a bare stage in a Broadway theater, seventeen dancers audition for a chorus line. The stories and songs they perform are based on interviews with Broadway dancers about their life experiences and relationships to dance. The musical became one of the longest-running shows in Broadway history and was hailed for its frank presentation of the dancers' stories. Issues of racial identity were prominent in these interviews and featured in the musical; however, certain aspects of race would be strategically excised when perceived to detract from the overall vision of director and co-choreographer Michael Bennett and composer Marvin Hamlisch. The racial experiences of the characters, while acknowledged as important, thus ultimately became eclipsed by a more universalized vision of the chorus line, both in the show's development and in its final narrative content.

A Chorus Line foregrounds a patently multicultural cast in its opening introductions of dancers. Richie (Ron Dennis) declares: "I was born on a full moon on June 13, 1948, and I'm black," a remark designed to draw audience laughter. Diana (Priscilla Lopez) began with: "My name is Diana Morales and I didn't change it because I figured ethnic was in." Connie (Baayork Lee) also emphasized her "ethnic" name as well as the fact that she is American born: "Connie Wong. It's always been Connie Wong. I was born in Chinatown—Lower East Side." Details of racial identity matter in other scenes as well. In "Nothing," Diana relates a bad classroom experience she had with Mr. Karp, her acting teacher. When Karp faults her for lack of emotional expression in an improvisational acting exercise about riding a bobsled, she defends herself with, "Hey, it's only the first week./ Maybe it's genetic. They don't have bobsleds in San Juan!" After Karp's criticisms, she prays to "Santa Maria" for guidance, and then hears a helpful voice telling her "This man is nothing!"[30]

Paul (Sammy Williams) also identifies himself as Puerto Rican. Based on stories told by Nicholas Dante, who was born Conrado Morales,[31] Paul's monologue begins with changing his name to sound Italian ("I, ah—just wanted to be somebody new, so I became Paul San Marco"). He seeks to escape his ethnic background ("What do Puerto Ricans know about theater? Now they have Channel Forty-Seven—but then they didn't have anything" [49]) and fears his immigrant Catholic family's discovery of his gay identity. He hides his work in a drag show from his parents, but they encounter him at the theater just as he is getting ready to go onstage. "Well, we were doing this oriental number and I looked like Anna May Wong. I had these two great big chrysanthemums on either side of my head for the finale and going down the stairs and who should I see standing by the stage door . . . my parents. They got there too early" (51). His monologue ends in a moving recognition scene in which his father then tells the producer to take care of his son.

A Chorus Line avoided stereotypical assumptions that its Black dancers would share the most tragic stories. In the initial workshops, dancer Candy Brown found herself as an outlier both racially and personally.

As usual, it was annoying, such a big group and I was the only black person there. But at the same time, ... it was beautiful that everybody just opened up so much. I mean the stories—oh, my God, I was stunned. In fact I felt like I was the disappointing one. I said, I know they think I'm from some ghetto and I got all these troubles, and I didn't. I had probably the most all-American, wonderful, happy life anybody could ever want. I was a cheerleader. I was in the choir. And all these broken homes and drunken parents, and I'm just in tears through all these stories. People ran away from home to dance and all that. My parents were so happy that I was doing *something* that they didn't care.[32]

Brown's "all-American" stories became the basis for the character of Richie, first played by Ron Dennis. According to Dennis, Brown was "one of a few African-American people who went to an all white school. She was in everything—choir, newspaper, sports. She was always trying to play everything, saying, 'Gimme the ball, gimme the ball.' Nobody would give it to her."[33] Richie's high-energy song "Gimme the Ball" had personal meaning for both Brown and Dennis. Like Brown, Dennis resisted contributing what he called "ghetto" stories to *A Chorus Line*. He later recalled that in the development process, "Some of the people at that last callback really laid out some heavy stories about the hurt of studying dance and all that, and I felt too much joy dancing to care about all that other bullshit."[34] Dennis wrote the music for "Gimme the Ball," which made use of improvisational and virtuosic melodies, syncopated rhythms, and gospel call-

and-response, and was the only number not composed by Hamlisch.

Other cast members also found their racial identities inextricable from their experiences of *A Chorus Line*. Chuck Cissel told a story of a previous unsuccessful audition with Bennett for the Sondheim musical *Follies*. Cissel recalled, "Michael told me that since *Follies* was a period piece, it would not be proper for this little black face to be onstage dancing. I was terribly hurt because I had outdanced all of those guys and then outsang them and outread them."[35] When he was later cast in *A Chorus Line*, he channeled these negative experiences to inform his character's relationship with Zach, the intimidating director.

> When we go to auditions and we are better, a lot of times we are not chosen because of our color. I was giving black people something to relate to. Every dancer who came to the show said, "Right on." Michael liked it, too, because it did give Zach something to play with. It's: "I know this step. Don't tell me what to do."

However, *A Chorus Line* backed away from calling too much attention to both cultural difference and racism in the musical theater industry. For instance, a verse sung partly in Spanish was excised from the final version of Diana Morales's song "Nothing."[36] The character of Connie presented a unique opportunity to feature an Asian American dancer, as illustrated by the Broadway casting of Baayork Lee, Lauren Kayahara, Janet Wong, Cynthia Onrubia, Lauren Tom, Lily-Lee Wong, and Sachi Shimizu.[37] That Connie is Asian American adds poignancy to her childhood realization that

"I was never gonna be Maria Tallchief" (the first Native American prima ballerina and a role model for many dancers of color). However, the role of Connie was cut to a bare minimum and its racial commentary largely effaced. In the appendix to the acting edition of the musical, the script advises a possible name change to "Connie Edna Mae Sue MacKenzie" for a non-Asian performer, with Connie's reference to performing in *The King and I* changed to appearing in "summer stock" (76, 78).

Ron Dennis noted that both his and Baayork Lee's roles in *A Chorus Line* were rendered "inconsequential" for audience members:

> The subsidiary characters were not being delved into enough for people to get a sense about Baayork as a very short Oriental or me as a Black. They got that Priscilla [Lopez, who played Diana] was Puerto Rican, that Sammy [Williams, who played Paul] was gay, that Donna was a soon-to-be star making a comeback, Sheila was a bitch—and Richie was a nonentity. He was there, but what character was he, was he Black? Now I laugh at it, but I used to get infuriated. Invariably it was someone white; never a Black person. Black people knew.[38]

Songs originally intended for Richie and Connie were cut entirely from the musical. "Confidence," a duet intended for Richie and Connie to sing about their common experience of being tokenized, was a unique opportunity to stage the tensions between an Asian American and a Black character as they compete for the one spot given to a "minority." The lyrics of this excised song emphasized the particular constraints on Asian American performers, as Connie's character sings about the different racial roles she has done: ("I've passed for Ethel Merman's little girlie, I've also done a year or two in *Purlie*"). [39]

> **Richie** He might take Suzy Wong but what do I know?
> **Connie** I might have trouble with a straight albino.
> **Both** Frig it!

The song was cut ostensibly because it was set to too cheerful a musical tune. Another unused song "Token" was likewise suggestive of Richie and Connie's casting predicaments, with lyrics describing "a new dance that's sweepin' the country/ From Chinatown to Watts" called "The Token." [40] Baayork Lee, who contributed much to the musical's choreography and was dance captain for the original production, commented that although the gradual reduction of her role as Connie didn't bother her at first, years later she questioned "How come I didn't get those lines? I could have done it." She then began to doubt herself, "Well, maybe he [Michael Bennett] didn't think I was talented enough." [41]

A Chorus Line simultaneously placed the racial identities of its dancers on display but downplayed the racism they face in their careers. Experiences of racial discrimination became eclipsed by the other challenges dancers face. Furthermore, individual distinctions, including those of race, were erased by *A Chorus Line*'s spectacular finale. As the dancers emerged in resplendent gold costume to sing "One," their racial differences mattered even less. Like their many chorus line predecessors, they become absorbed into a traditional kickline. Race became a means of highlighting each of its dancers' unique stories. But in the end, differences were downplayed in favor of a more race-neutral version of the chorus line. As the musical unfolds, race springs briefly into the spotlight but then becomes effaced in favor of a harmonious vision of dancing bodies moving as one.

Notes

1. Richard Rodgers, Oscar Hammerstein, and Joseph Fields, *Flower Drum Song: A Musical Play* (Farrar, Straus, and Cudahy, 1959), 87–8.

2. Derek and Julia Parker, *The Natural History of the Chorus Girl* (Indianapolis, IN: Bobbs-Merrill, 1975), 55.

3. *New York Times*, September 5, 1909, 9.

4. David R. Roediger, *The Wages of Whiteness: Race and the Making of the American Working Class* (London: Verso, 1999), 116.

5. Richard and Paulette Ziegfeld, *The Ziegfeld Touch, The Life and Times of Florenz Ziegfeld* (New York: Harry N. Abrams, Inc., 1993), 33.

6. Linda Mizejewski, *Ziegfeld Girl: Image and Icon in Culture and Cinema* (Durham, NC: Duke University Press, 1999), 11.

7. *Ziegfeld Touch*, 41.

8. *Ziegfeld Touch*, 239.

9. Mizejewski, *Ziegfeld Girl*, 8; *Ziegfeld Touch*, 250.

10. *Ziegfeld Touch*, 250.

11. Doris Eaton Travis, Joseph and Charles Eaton, and J. R. Morris, *The Days We Danced: The Story of My Theatrical*

Family From Florenz Ziegfeld to Arthur Murray and Beyond (Seattle: Marquand, 2003), 67.

12. Mizejewski, *Ziegfeld Girl*, 93.

13. Mizejewski, *Ziegfeld Girl*, 24.

14. James Weldon Johnson, *Black Manhattan* (originally published 1930; reprint New York: Arno, 1967), 95.

15. Quoted in Thomas L. Riis, *Just Before Jazz: Black Musical Theater in New York 1890-1915* (Washington, DC: Smithsonian Press, 1989), 137.

16. Jayna Brown, *Babylon Girls: Black Women Performers and the Shaping of the Modern* (Durham, NC: Duke University Press, 2008), 108.

17. Brenda Dixon Gottschild, *Waltzing in the Dark: African American Vaudeville and Race Politics in the Swing Era* (New York: St. Martin's, 2000), 135.

18. Irving Zeidman, *The American Burlesque Show* (New York: Hawthorn Books, 1967), 43.

19. Al Rose, *Eubie Blake* (New York: Shirmer, 1979), 78.

20. Sissle, Noble, and Eubie Blake, *Shuffle Along,* edited by Lyn Schenbeck and Lawrence Schenbeck (American Musicological Society. Middleton, WI: A-R Editions, Inc. 2018), 113–19.

21. Review of "Shuffle Along," *New York Herald,* May 24, 1921.

22. *Chicago Herald Examiner*, February 18, 1922.

23. John Martin, New York *Dramatic Mirror* and *Theater World*, August 27, 1921; quoted in Marshall and Jean Stearns, *Jazz Dance: The Story of American Vernacular Dance* (New York: Da Capo Press, 1994), 141.

24. New York *Globe*, August 24, 1921; quoted Stearns, *Jazz Dance*, 141.

25. *Ziegfeld Touch*, 59.

26. Stearns, *Jazz Dance*, 130.

27. Hirsch, Louis A., Gene Buck, and Dave Stamper. Music Division, The New York Public Library. "It's Getting Dark on Old Broadway," *The New York Public Library Digital Collections*, 1922, https://digitalcollections.nypl.org/items /70cb8fd2-3a86-325f-e040-e00a180662f3.

28. *Ziegfeld Touch*, 254.

29. Saidiya Hartman, *Wayward Lives, Beautiful Experiments: Intimate Histories of Riotous Black Girls, Troublesome Women, and Queer Radicals* (New York: Norton & Co., 2019), 305.

30. *A Chorus Line*, conceived and originally directed and choreographed by Michael Bennett, book by James Kirkwood and Nicholas Dante, music by Marvin Hamlisch, and lyrics by Edward Kleban (New York: Tams, 1985, 1975), 33–4. Subsequent page numbers appear parenthetically.

31. Alberto Sandoval-Sánchez, *José, Can You See? Latinos On and Off Broadway* (The University of Wisconsin Press, 1999), 83.

32. Denny Martin Flinn, *What They Did for Love: The Untold Story behind the Making of a Chorus Line* (New York: Bantam Books 1989), 34–5.

33. Gary Stevens and Alan George, *The Longest Line* (New York: Applause 1995), 85.

34. Flinn, *What They Did for Love*, 68.

35. Flinn, *What They Did for Love*, 75.

36. Robert Viagas, Baayork Lee, and Thommie Walsh, *On the Line: The Creation of a Chorus Line,* (New York: William Morrow and Co., 1990), 197.

37. Stevens and George, *The Longest Line*, 228.

38. Viagas, Lee, and Walsh, *On the Line*, 216–17.

39. Quoted in Warren Hoffman, *The Great White Way: Race and the Broadway Musical* (Rutgers University Press, 2014), 154.

40. Hoffman, *The Great White Way*, 155.

41. Viagas, Lee, and Walsh, *On the Line*, 196–7.

5
Who Tells Your Story?
Race, Immigration, and the American Dream

Historian Erika Lee has pointed out that although the United States is sometimes celebrated as a "nation of immigrants" offering a haven for some new arrivals, it is also a "nation of xenophobia" that deports and discriminates against others.[1] Valued for their hard work and entrepreneurial spirit, "good" immigrants are embraced into American dreams of belonging and success. "Bad" immigrants, on the other hand, are stigmatized as troublemakers competing for jobs and reducing neighborhoods to crime.

In US law, race and national origin shaped this distinction between "good" and "bad" immigrants. The Naturalization Act of 1790 granted citizenship to "free white person[s] . . . of good character," excluding enslaved Africans, free Blacks (though some states allowed them citizenship at the state level), indentured servants, and Native Americans. In 1868, the Fourteenth Amendment extended citizenship to people of African descent born in the United States but exempted Native Americans living on reservations. The Naturalization Act of 1870 extended naturalization to those born in Africa but denied naturalized citizenship to those born in China. The Chinese Exclusion Act of 1882 and subsequent Asian exclusion laws set race-based limits on immigration and naturalization, and was followed by the 1924 Immigration Act, which likewise reflected racial and ethnic biases.

Musicals such as *Finian's Rainbow* (1947), *The Most Happy Fella* (1956), and *Ragtime* (1977) suggest how even "good" immigrants struggle to adapt to American life. The distinction between "good" and "bad" immigrants figures more prominently in *West Side Story* (1957). While *West Side Story* portrays both white and Puerto Rican characters as involved in gang warfare, the European ethnic backgrounds of the Jets are subsumed into whiteness while the Puerto Rican Sharks are portrayed as Spanish-speaking and culturally foreign. The Sharks and their girlfriends voice their discontent with life in the United States in the song "America." Rosalia remembers Puerto Rico as a "lovely island" with "tropical breezes," but to Anita it is an "ugly island" of tropical diseases, hurricanes, and overpopulation. Anita prefers "the island Manhattan" and is joined by a female chorus claiming that "Life is all right in America," while their boyfriends retort "If you're all-white in America."[2]

West Side Story had a lasting impact on many, among them a young Lin-Manuel Miranda. Seeing the 1961 movie for the first time, he was struck by its portrayal of Puerto Rican New Yorkers as well as the casting of Rita Morena as Anita, calling it a "gamechanger."[3] But like others who criticize *West*

Side Story's lack of cultural authenticity,[4] Miranda is aware of "bad" immigrant stereotypes. Alberto Sandoval-Sánchez comments on how the musical presents Puerto Ricans as "a threat to the U.S. national order," as consistent with other stereotypes fostered by American theater and film of Latin men as "illegal aliens, criminals, gangsters, and drug addicts" or at best "gracious Latin lovers," and Latinas as the "vamp, seductress, or spitfire."[5]

Miranda's 2005 musical *In the Heights* (with book by Quiara Alegría Hudes) openly challenges these representations. In a 2008 YouTube parody of "One Day More" from *Les Miserables*, the original Broadway cast of *In the Heights* sings that their show can be summed up as "Twenty-three Latinos in the Broadway show/Not a lot of drugs, not a lot of crime/Not a lot of write-up in the *New York Times*."[6] Most of its characters are hard-working and entrepreneurial. Washington Heights bodega owner Usnavi, who hails from the Dominican Republic, worries about providing his customers with the right kind of coffee. Puerto Rican immigrants Kevin and Camila Rosario own a local cab company, and Daniela, Carla, and Vanessa work at a beauty salon. When their daughter Nina, a first-generation college student, announces that she has lost her Stanford University scholarship and plans to drop out, the Rosarios are aghast, and her father impetuously sells the cab company to pay her tuition.

The characters are model immigrants whose hard work and devotion to family allow their American-born children to assimilate, have access to education, and find professional success. But the musical also comments on how initiative and hard work do not always result in upward mobility. In "Paciencia y Fe" (Patience and Faith), Abuela Claudia, the surrogate grandmother of the neighborhood, laments how "fresh off the boat," she and her mother were exploited as domestic workers "scrubbing the whole of the upper East Side."[7] Their patience and faith help them survive, but Abuela Claudia wonders whether their struggle is worth the cost. After discovering that she has won the lottery, her mixed feelings make it clear that it is only the lucky ticket, not her mother's dutiful labor, that yields a chance at the American Dream.

Washington Heights is portrayed as home to successive generations of immigrants, as the Rosarios reminiscence about buying the car service from "Mr. O'Hanrahan" when "half this block was Irish" (133). But the musical reminds audiences that racial distinctions still matter in shaping immigrant aspirations. Nina's love interest Benny is Black (but not Afro-Latino), and Kevin expresses disapproval with "Do you think you're anywhere close to her level?" When Benny replies, "We're not that different," Kevin angrily responds, "You know nothing about our culture!" and "You will never be a part of this family, entiendes?" (109–10). While not directly called out as racism, this comment might suggest a degree of anti-Blackness as well as elitism inherent in Kevin's reservations.[8]

Even though characters such as Kevin see themselves as "good" immigrants aspiring to white gentility, their lives remain precarious due to gentrification in Washington Heights. In the opening scene, Usnavi raps of the "tough" times on his bodega and how his neighbors have started "packin' up and pickin' up" (3). The small frozen-ice business of Piragua Man must compete with the large ice cream franchise Mister Softee. Daniela and Vanessa tell Nina that their salon is moving to the Bronx because the rent has gotten too high. The reggaeton-inspired song "96,000" registers their dreams of wealth, status, and leisure. Daniela wants a "brand-new lease" in "Atlantic City with a Malibu Breeze," Vanessa plans to move downtown to "a nice studio" that will allow her to leave the "barrio," and Benny fantasizes about becoming a businessman (47–59). However, Usnavi's young cousin Sonny imagines a different use for the windfall, providing computers and education for neighborhood youth. Sonny's alternative dream changes the terms of success in America from individual mobility to community aid.

Sonny's dream and Abuela Claudia's nurturing presence support a vision of neighborhood community. A vibrant mix of different cultures, Washington Heights is nonetheless not pictured as an exotic tourist destination. As Sandoval-Sanchez describes, Anglo-American popular culture has made clichés out of Spanish phrases such as "sí sí," hasta mañana," "chiquita," "señorita," and "fiesta," and appropriated Latin rhythms, music, and dance to endow white culture with "primitivism, liberation of the instincts and the body, and pervasive sexuality."[9] In contrast, *In the Heights* uses Spanish to honor both bilingual characters and audience members. Similarly, Latin rhythms of 3-2 clave, and rhythms of Afro-Caribbean and Latin music such as salsa, bolero, and regaetton are used to evoke what is local and familiar rather than foreign. Musical numbers such as the merengue-inspired "Carnaval de Barrio" emphasize the characters' own ethnic sensibilities. The different flags displayed prominently on the set serve not just as colorful decorations but as signals of strong transnational ties. Importantly, the distinct identities of the characters support a sense of pan-ethnic and multiracial solidarity that is unique to the United States. Carla, for instance, identifies with her Dominican and Cuban mother and Chilean and Puerto Rican father, jubilantly proclaiming herself "Chile-domini-curican" and adding "but I always say I'm from Queens!" (118).

Community caregiving is played out in different musical numbers as Benny and Nina direct cabdrivers through New York City traffic ("Benny's Dispatch"), as Daniela and Carla enjoy the gossipy rituals of hair and nail salons ("No Me Diga" [You Don't Say]), and as the Piragua Guy sells frozen treats on a hot summer day ("Piragua"). While New York City is understood to be prohibitively expensive, Washington Heights is imagined as a place of comfort, with familiar faces, food, and small luxuries such as sweet coffee, refreshing piraguas, or open hydrants and cool breezes on a hot day. The ending of *In the Heights* affirms local immigrant communities as quintessentially American. Rather than leaving Washington Heights for a more leisurely life in the Dominican Republic, Usnavi continues to run his bodega, taking on Abuela Claudia's role as the keeper of neighborhood history. He tells the audience that he is "a streetlight" who "illuminate[s] the stories of the people in the street" and declares jubilantly that "I'm home!/Where people come, people go!/Let me show all of these people what I know, that's there's no place like home!" while other members of the cast reaffirm "We're home!" (151–3).

Running Out of Time: *Hamilton: An American Musical*

Hamilton: An American Musical (2015) explores the life of Alexander Hamilton, a founding father so influential in building the political and economic foundations of the country that he is commemorated on the US ten-dollar bill. Different scenes follow Hamilton's coming to New York as an orphaned teenager from the island of Nevis in the Caribbean (then part of the British West Indies), marriage to Elizabeth (Eliza) Schuyler, service as an aide to General George Washington during the Revolutionary War, lobbying for a stronger constitution and centralized federal government, appointment as the first US Secretary of the Treasury, and death in 1804 in a duel with political rival Aaron Burr. But like any musical, *Hamilton* speaks to the moment in which it was written as much as it does any past time period. The show uses multiracial casting and raises contemporary questions about the distinction between "good" and "bad" immigrants and the dangers of buying into systems of power and privilege at the expense of family and self.

Productions of *Hamilton* have featured mainly Black, Latinx, and Asian American actors in its leading roles. Jeremy McCarter hails the "revolution of the show itself: a musical that changes the way that Broadway sounds, that alters who gets to tell the story of our founding, that lets us glimpse the new, more diverse America rushing our way."[10] McCarter and others have praised the casting as the musical's most radical move. Featuring actors whose racial identities have been stereotyped, appropriated, or erased in the past shows, as Donatella Galella has suggested, "a more inclusive

United States where revolutionary history can belong to U.S. Americans of color."[11] This sensibility is registered in the music and choreography, which uses Black-inflected rap, hip hop, R&B, and soul styles as well as pop and show tunes. For some, *Hamilton* illustrates racial progress both on and off the stage; for instance, in *Rolling Stone*, Richard Morgan called Miranda "the everyman we need to re-write the American Dream."[12]

Miranda defines his protagonist Hamilton through historical quotations in which the real Alexander Hamilton declared, "I am a stranger in this country. I have no property here, no connexions [*sic*]" and posed the question, "Am I then more of an American than those who drew their first breath on American ground?" (13, 147). Miranda's Hamilton epitomizes "good" immigrant qualities such as ingenuity, pluck, and discipline. In the opening number, Burr asks "How does a bastard, orphan, son of a whore and a/ Scotsman . . . Grow up to be a hero and a scholar?" John Laurens responds that though Hamilton was a "ten-dollar Founding Father without a father," he "got a lot farther by working a lot harder/ By being a lot smarter/By being a self-starter." By the end of the song, Hamilton is pictured as standing on "a ship headed for the new land," destined for New York, where "you can be a new man" (16–17). Hamilton declares in "My Shot" that "I'm just like my country/ I'm young, scrappy and hungry" (26), emphasizing the initiative and work ethic that is considered important to success in America.

Emphasizing Hamilton as a "good" immigrant challenged the conservative anti-immigrant sentiments of the early 2000s, an era that saw increasingly stringent border policing and deportation as well as political measures to restrict Muslim immigrants and refugees.[13] After their victorious military strategy in the Battle of Yorktown in 1781, Frenchman Lafayette and Caribbean-born Hamilton exchange high-fives. In many performances their line, "Immigrants: We get the job done," prompted pro-immigrant cheers and applause from the audience, so much so that Miranda added extra bars "just to absorb the reaction."[14] But *Hamilton* also questions models of immigrant belonging in which all new settlers in the United States easily prove themselves worthy of national acceptance. At various points, the idea of Hamilton as the "good immigrant"—hard-working, upwardly mobile, and bound for assimilation—is placed in tension with his Otherness. In "Washington on Your Side," Jefferson, Madison, and Burr team up against Hamilton, complaining, "This immigrant isn't somebody we chose . . . . This immigrant's keeping us all on our toes" (200).

The musical links anti-immigrant sentiment with racism, as later in the musical John Adams calls Hamilton "a creole bastard" (224), a line based on the real Adams calling Hamilton "a bastard brat of a Scotch pedlar." While the character of Hamilton is not understood to be Black; the musical makes him a champion for enslaved Africans. Miranda was inspired by Ron Chernow's 2004 biography of Alexander Hamilton, which called him an "uncompromising abolitionist,"[15] and references Hamilton's antislavery essays as well as his association with South Carolina statesman John Laurens. Laurens had proposed to recruit a military brigade of slaves by promising them freedom (a plan that was defeated by political opposition in South Carolina). In "My

Shot," Laurens and Hamilton declare "We'll never be free" until slavery is abolished, but Laurens is killed during the last phase of the Revolutionary War. At the end of *Hamilton*, Eliza says that she is continuing Hamilton's legacy by speaking out against slavery, suggesting that he would have done more had he not been killed in his duel with Burr.

However, depictions of Hamilton as an uncompromising abolitionist are at odds with historical evidence of Hamilton's participation in the slave trade and his family's ownership of slaves.[16] The musical does briefly acknowledge this contradiction in the opening number "Alexander Hamilton." Laurens and Jefferson describe how at age fourteen, Hamilton was placed "in charge of a trading charter" and "every day while slaves were being slaughtered and carted," he "struggled and kept his guard up." Hamilton has an immediate familiarity with slavery but is distanced from these early experiences as he becomes "another immigrant,/ comin' up from the bottom" (16–17) in the United States.

Wind Dell Woods has commented that *Hamilton*'s Black casting and use of hip hop provide an illusion of interracial solidarity that masks Hamilton's complicity with slavery as well as the dispossession and genocide of Native Americans in colonial America. Woods calls out the musical's "ethical dilemma" insofar that its casting and evocation of Black music "structurally and symbolically conflates the peculiar position of the black captive population with that of immigrant populations," when in fact "the erasure of the black captive and indigenous population" was "the condition of possibility for the American immigrant narrative to emerge."[17] This critique rightly points out the irony of Hamilton being seen as a champion of abolitionism when he is celebrated as a "good" immigrant, a formulation predicated on the exploitation of enslaved labor and colonization of Indigenous lands by white settlers. Yet it is important to keep in mind that *Hamilton* also questions aspects of this quintessentially American success.

In the Heights celebrates the hard work of "good" immigrants but points out that the American Dream rewards only a privileged few. Washington Heights is both a place of economic struggle and a haven offering communal forms of support and sustenance. In contrast, most scenes of *Hamilton* revolve around antagonism and violence as characters compete to be in "the room where it happens." This masculine milieu requires constant demonstrations of military prowess, intellectual accomplishment, and assertiveness. Hamilton's success is tied to his relentless work ethic. In "Non-stop," Burr questions "Why do you write like you're running out of time?" (137) and this question is repeated throughout the musical. While Hamilton's ambition and need for external validation motivate him, they become his fatal flaws as achievement turns into excess, and Hamilton neglects his marriage and family.

The Schuyler sisters, Angelica and Eliza, balance out Hamilton's character in important ways. In developing these two female characters, Miranda strategically alters a historical timeline in which the real-life Angelica Schuyler had already eloped with John Barker Church before meeting Hamilton. However, Miranda has an unmarried Angelica fall in love with a penniless Hamilton. In "Satisfied," Hamilton and Angelica are presented as kindred restless spirits, both of whom "will never be satisfied" (85). But Angelica gives up her romantic feelings for Hamilton not only to preserve her family's social status but also because she knows that her sister Eliza has feelings for him. Angelica later supports her sister after Eliza is devastated by Hamilton's extra-marital affair with Maria Reynolds.

The character of Eliza presents an even more significant contrast to Hamilton's self-absorption. The wealthy Schuyler family had many more privileges than did Hamilton, who needed to be a "self-starter." However, Eliza's lack of ambition does not just come from her class privilege. Her character offers a vision of quiet contentment that is at odds with the constant striving of the male characters as well as Angelica's marrying for status. In "That would be enough," she reprises an optimistic line from an earlier song, "The Schuyler Sisters," by asking Hamilton to "look around" and marvel at "how lucky we are to be alive right now." She then tells Hamilton "We don't need a legacy" and describes her wish that he could have "peace of mind" in their relationship together: "And I could be enough/ And we could be enough./That would be enough" (110). Her repetition of the word "enough" speaks to her placid nature, but also offers a compelling vision of how life could be otherwise meaningful.

In the final scene, Eliza puts her own public contributions on a par with Hamilton's accomplishments. In "Who Lives, Who Dies, Who Tells Your Story," she tells the audience that following Hamilton's death, "I put myself back in the narrative," and stops "wasting time on tears" (280). She details not only her efforts to compile Hamilton's biography and continue his antislavery work but also what she is proudest of—her efforts to establish the first private orphanage in

New York City. Eliza thus transforms the terms of what counts as success by pointing to her own legacy of nurturing hundreds of children. Significantly, she is no longer content with her earlier vision of family life as "enough," but instead asserts how these projects cannot be completed within her lifetime—"I live another fifty years./ It's not enough." If Hamilton exemplified the immense accomplishments of a founding father, Eliza frames herself as a "founding mother" whose contributions center on the care and nurture of family and community. The ending thus shifts from how Hamilton is remembered—for his military and political leadership and building of the young country's financial system—to Eliza's work, which involves a different kind of self-sacrifice. The question that the audience is left with is not just how to tell the story of Alexander Hamilton, but whether contributions such as those of Eliza will be commemorated in the public eye, as she asks "And when my time is up?/ Have I done enough?/ Will they tell my story?" (281).

Hamilton highlights how the tensions between individual achievement and communal cooperation affect how we might read Hamilton's immigrant story. If Hamilton is pictured as sacrificing family for reputation, his excesses might be seen as the direct result of his being labeled a "bad" immigrant and trying to prove himself to be "good." In the song "Wait for It," Burr describes Hamilton as someone who "exhibits no restraint" or hesitation, saying "He takes and he takes and he takes" (92). But as Burr describes, Hamilton's behavior is shaped by his outsider status: "Hamilton faces an endless uphill climb . . . He has something to prove/He has nothing to lose." Even as Hamilton might be seen as an immigrant hero, his rise does little to challenge the hierarchical, sexist, and meritocratic structures that bring some individuals to the top but fail to make everyone equal. It is Eliza, then, who defines a different set of goals for success, ending the musical with an alternative vision of what the American Dream might entail when directed less toward individual gain and more toward common good.

Conclusion: Philippa Soo in *Hamilton*

Reflecting the politics of the early twenty-first century in which it was first written and performed, *Hamilton* casts Black, Latinx, and Asian American actors in most of its major roles. This shows how performers of color can convincingly embody characters known mainly from history books. It also demonstrates how history can be presented less as a factual account of what actually happened, than as a set of imagined "what if?" possibilities. This book began by discussing the problems that occur when character types, casting practices, or narratives are repeated. *Hamilton*, in contrast, allows for stories to be retold in new ways.

This book's objectives have been to provide historical context, emphasize multiracial and comparative perspectives, and encourage critical reflection on American musical theater. With these three objectives in mind, we will examine one final example from *Hamilton*: the original Broadway production's casting of the Chinese American actress Phillipa Soo as Eliza. At first glance, this choice functioned somewhat differently than did the casting of Black and Latinx actors, whose presence highlighted the musical's explicit commentary on slavery and immigration. *Hamilton* makes no reference to orientalism during Hamilton's life, though historians have provided us with compelling evidence that eighteenth-century Americans were fascinated with Asia and China in particular.[18] Known for her nuanced and evocative vocal and acting abilities, the biracial Soo easily captured the imagination of audiences as a white character. Her casting thus begs the question of why it really matters to have an Asian American performer in this role.

As noted earlier, Asian Americans have been relatively rare on Broadway, and Soo's performance was hailed as a welcome instance of racial visibility in American theater. But it also added another dimension to the musical's commentary on immigrant identity and the American Dream. In the late nineteenth century, anti-Asian sentiment and the legal exclusion of Chinese immigrants redefined the United States as a "gate-keeping" nation policing its borders. Asian immigrants have been perceived as both "bad" and "good" immigrants, imagined as both the villainous "yellow peril" and hard-working, high-achieving "model minorities."[19] Moreover, in works such as *Madama Butterfly* or *Miss Saigon*, Asian women have been repeatedly typecast as submissive and docile love interests.

The musical shows Hamilton writing to Eliza before his fatal duel, calling her "Best of wives and best of women" (269), a phrase taken from Alexander Hamilton's letters. These compliments reveal the potential for gendered and racialized typecasting, insofar that Eliza might be viewed as a traditionally subordinate, feminine role. Casting an Asian

American actress such as Soo thus risks reinvigorating both the stereotypes of the hyperfeminine "Butterfly" and the overachieving model minority. Thus it is important to note that Soo played Eliza with decisiveness and agency, removing herself and reinserting herself back into public life. Soo's Eliza also interrupts Hamilton's excessive adulation of work with a gentle but firm "enough." Casting an Asian American actress accentuated how the character of Eliza might fit—and yet resist—reduction to the "best of wives and best of women." This revolutionary yet nuanced casting choice prompts us to think harder about the complex ways in which race matters in theatrical perception and representation.

Theater makers and audiences alike have become increasingly aware of the power of even one actor, one gesture, or one song to make a difference in perception. On May 25, 2020, the murder of George Floyd by Minneapolis police took place during the Covid pandemic. Floyd's brutal death, one in the long line of many tragedies, gave significant new momentum to protests of anti-Black racism. What were sometimes called the twin pandemics of racism and Covid had an unprecedented impact on professional theater in the United States. Two months prior to Floyd's death, theaters on Broadway had already shut down due to Covid. When theaters returned to Broadway, there were numerous calls for changes, both dramatic and subtle, to popular musicals. In *Hamilton*, the dancer playing Sally Hemings, the enslaved woman who bore Thomas Jefferson multiple children, now pointedly turned her back on Jefferson during the second act. In *The Lion King*, references to a "monkey" character, played by an African American woman, were now excised.

The creative team behind *The Book of Mormon*, Matt Stone, Trey Parker, and Robert Lopez, met with the cast to rework significant moments in the musical's satirical plot and staging. Significantly, in many cases it was the actors themselves, who lobbied for change. A July 2020 letter from actors who had been appearing in *The Book of Mormon* warned that "When the show returns, all of our work will be viewed through a new lens."[20]

This "new lens" has made the many complex issues of race in American musical theater even more worth examining in depth. Now more than ever, both historical knowledge and critical examination should inform and enhance the experience of American musical theater. Increasing social awareness and action on the part of artists, performers, and audiences bodes well for a future in which musical theater helps to build meaningful human connection and contribute to racial justice. It is my hope that this book will help with this ongoing process.

Notes

1. Erika Lee, *America for Americans: A History of Xenophobia in the United States* (New York: Basic Books, 2019, repr. 2021), 20–1.

2. Stephen Sondheim, *Finishing the Hat: Collected Lyrics (1954–1981) with Attendant Comments, Heresies, Principles, Grudges, Whines, and Anecdotes* (New York: Knopf, 2010), 42.

3. "Lin-Manuel Miranda on his First Viewing of 'West Side Story,'" *PBS American Masters*, https://www.pbs.org/wnet/

americanmasters/lin-manuel-miranda-his-first-viewing-west
-side-story-jroswl/18863/ (Accessed June 13, 2022).

4. Yura Sapi, "The *West Side Story* Appropriation We Never
   Really Talk About," *Howl Round*, August 25, 2017, https://
   howlround.com/west-side-story-appropriation-we-never
   -really-talk-about.

5. Alberto Sandoval-Sánchez, *José, Can You See? Latinos On and Off
   Broadway* (The University of Wisconsin Press, 1999), 27–8.

6. The twenty-second annual Easter Bonnet Competition,
   fundraiser for Broadway Cares/Equity Fights AIDS,
   April 28 and 29, 2008, https://www.youtube.com/watch?v
   =4G4Qvjv5W2c.

7. Lin-Manuel Miranda and Quiara Alegría Hudes, *In the
   Heights* (New York: Applause, 2006), 63. Subsequent page
   numbers appear parenthetically.

8. The 2021 film version of *In the Heights* omitted this dialogue,
   and the film's casting of relatively few dark-skinned Afro-
   Latinx actors lead to concerns about its failure to acknowledge
   anti-Black colorism within Latin communities. This elicited
   an apology from Miranda. Julia Jacobs, "Lin-Manuel Miranda
   addresses 'In the Heights' Casting Criticism," *New York Times*,
   June 15, 2021.

9. Sandoval-Sánchez, *José, Can You See?*, 31.

10. McCarter, "Introduction," in *Hamilton the Revolution*, edited
    by Lin-Manuel Miranda and Jeremy McCarter (New York:
    Grand Center Publishing, Hachette Book Group, 2016), 10.
    Subsequent page numbers appear parenthetically.

11. Donatella Galella, "Being in 'The Room Where It Happens':
    Hamilton, Obama, and Nationalist Neoliberal Multicultural

Inclusion," *Theater Survey*, vol. 59, no. 3 (September 2018): 363–85, 370.

12. Richard Morgan, "Why 'Hamilton' Star Lin-Manuel Miranda Is Better Than Perfect," *Rolling Stone*, May 3, 2016, https://www.rollingstone.com/music/music-news/why-hamilton-star-lin-manuel-miranda-is-better-than-perfect-68210/.

13. Galella, "Being in 'The Room Where It Happens,'" 373.

14. Miranda and McCarter 121, note 1.

15. Jennifer Schuessler, "Alexander Hamilton, Enslaver? New Research Says Yes," *New York Times*, November 9, 2020, https://www.nytimes.com/2020/11/09/arts/alexander-hamilton-enslaver-research.html.

16. Jessie Serfilippi, "'As Odious and Immoral a Thing': Alexander Hamilton's Hidden History as an Enslaver," Schuyler Mansion State Historic Site, New York State Office of Parks, Recreation, and Historic Preservation, 2020, https://parks.ny.gov/documents/historic-sites/SchuylerMansionAlexanderHamiltonsHiddenHistoryasanEnslaver.pdf.

17. Wind Dell Woods, "'Bonding over Phobia': Restaging a Revolution at the Expense of Black Revolt," in *Reframing the Musical: Race, Culture and Identity*, edited by Sarah Whitfield (London: Red Globe Press, 2019), 211–32, 222, 225.

18. See John Kuo Wei Tchen, *New York Before Chinatown: Orientalism and the Shaping of American Culture, 1776–1882* (Baltimore, MD: Johns Hopkins University Press, 2001).

19. For more background on Asian American history, see Erika Lee, *The Making of Asian Americans: A History* (New York: Simon and Schuster, 2016). For an overview of oriental typecasting in American theater, see Josephine Lee,

"Yellowface: Historical and Contemporary Contexts," in *The Oxford Encyclopedia of Asian American Literature and Culture* (New York: Oxford University Press, 2020), http://oxfordre .com/literature/view/10.1093/acrefore/9780190201098.001 .0001/acrefore-9780190201098-e-834.

20. Michael Paulson, "As Broadway Returns, Shows Rethink and Restage Depictions of Race," *New York Times*, October 23, 2021.

Index

INDEX